# THE APPRENTICESHIP

*The CBC International Service*
*History of Canada :*

**1.** The Ordeal of New France
(The French Colonial Period)
By W. J. Eccles, University of Toronto

**2.** Genesis of a Nation
(The British Colonial Period)
By Laurier LaPierre, McGill University

**3.** The Apprenticeship
(The Dominion of Canada's first half century)
By Laurier LaPierre, McGill University

**4.** The Coming of Age
(The modern era : 1914 to 1967)
By D. C. Masters, Guelph University

Each series consists of 13 half-hour radio programs

*13 RADIO SCRIPTS*

by

LAURIER L. LAPIERRE, PH.D.
*Department of History*
*McGill University*
*Montreal*

# THE APPRENTICESHIP

Canada from Confederation
to the eve of the First World War
Part 3 of a four-part history of Canada

THE CANADIAN BROADCASTING CORPORATION

*Printed in Canada for*

*CBC PUBLICATIONS BRANCH*
Box 500, Station A, Toronto 116
by Pierre Des Marais Inc

# INTRODUCTION

In 1963, when the 100th anniversary of Canada's nationhood was still four years in the future, the CBC International Service undertook to produce, as a Centennial project, fifty-two half-hour programs on the history of Canada.

By 1966 four series of thirteen programs each, covering the four main periods in Canadian history, had been produced by our Transcription Service, and broadcast on our own shortwave transmissions and by hundreds of radio stations in all parts of the world.

Never before had we offered our listeners such a lengthy series on a single subject. Individual programs and short series on various aspects of Canada have always been well received, but we could not be sure how this series would fare. However, the response was most gratifying. Immediately we began to receive requests from all parts of the world for copies of the scripts. Not only had our listeners enjoyed listening to the programs; they also wanted to read and study the material they had heard.

We therefore decided to publish the texts of the fifty-two programs in four volumes, corresponding to the four thirteen-part series outlined on page II. We hope that our readers will find these little books as interesting as our listeners have found the programs.

CHARLES R. DELAFIELD
*Director, CBC International Service*

# A NOTE ON THE TEXT

As these programs were intended for an audience of non-Canadian listeners the authors of all four series were asked to keep the scripts as simple as possible, avoiding side issues and details which might confuse the uninitiated listener. They were also asked to tell Canada's story as much as possible through readings from documents. We did not want fifty-two lectures.

These publications bear little resemblance, therefore, to textbooks on Canadian history. Admittedly they do not cover the subject as thoroughly, but we think that the main issues are developed rather more fully, and that the main personalities emerge more clearly. We even suspect that the typical Canadian student has a less vivid impression of, say, William Lyon Mackenzie or John A. Macdonald or Wilfrid Laurier than the radio listener in Hong Kong or San Francisco who has heard these men portrayed in their own words in these programs.

In preparing the scripts for publication we have restored certain passages which had to be deleted from the original versions in order to make the programs fit into the half-hour format. These passages are enclosed in square brackets.

The narrator in the recordings of *The Apprenticeship* was Budd Knapp. The documents were read by Henry Ramer, Paul Hébert, Paul Dupuis, Robert Christie, Howard Ryshpan, Percy Rodriguez, George Alexander, Philip Nielson, and Anthony Robinow. The discs are still available to radio stations outside Canada.

KENNETH S. MURPHY
*Producer, CBC International Service*

# CONTENTS

## "FROM SEA TO SEA" 1
### Rounding Out Confederation

On July 1st, 1867 the British North American colonies of Nova Scotia, New Brunswick, Canada East and Canada West* were joined together to form the Canadian Confederation — the Dominion of Canada.

The task had only begun. Like the United States, Canada was born in the east and grew towards the west. Consequently a map of Canada on July 1st, 1867, bears little resemblance to the map of Canada today. The vast area which is now the provinces of Manitoba, Saskatchewan, Alberta, and the northern

---

* The last two names are the source of much confusion, at first, to students of Canadian history. Under the provisions of the Constitutional Act of 1791, a British order-in-council divided France's former colony of Quebec, conquerered 31 years earlier, into two provinces, each with its own government : Lower Canada, the majority of whose inhabitants were descended from the original French colonists, and Upper Canada, populated mainly by Loyalist immigrants from the new United States following the American Revolution. By the Act of Union of 1840 the two colonies were reunited under a single government and renamed Canada East and Canada West, but the names Lower Canada and Upper Canada, respectively, continued to be used unofficially (as in the Newfoundlanders' petition on page 3). To add to the confusion, the Maritime Colonies were frequently referred to as the "Lower provinces". Canada East and Canada West entered Confederation in 1867 as the provinces of Quebec and Ontario. The reasons for, and consequences of, these changes are discussed in the previous volume of this series, *Genesis of a Nation*. — K.M.

parts of Ontario and Quebec, belonged in 1867 to the Hudson's Bay Company, and was known as the Northwest Territories. On the Pacific Ocean, the colony of British Columbia was still unconnected to the new Dominion, either physically or constitutionally.

So the task had only begun. In the years to come it would be necessary to link together people of diverse cultures, languages and religions, to develop an effective transportation system which would bring together scattered settlements, to acquire still privately-owned lands, and to devise economic policies which would ensure the prosperity of the whole country.

In 1867 the Fathers of Confederation had made an act of hope in an uncertain future. As George Brown, one of the leading Fathers, had said, as he begged his fellow countrymen to accept the terms of Confederation :

> The welfare for many years of four millions of people hangs on our decision. Shall we then rise to the occasion ? Shall we approach this discussion without partisanship, and free from every personal feeling but an earnest resolution to discharge conscientiously, the duty which, an over-ruling Providence has placed upon us ? It may be that some among us will yet live to see the day when as a result of this measure a great and powerful people may have grown up on these lands — when the boundless forests all around us shall have given way to smiling fields and thriving towns — and when one united government under the British flag shall extend from shore to shore.

One government to extend from sea to sea — *a mari usque ad mare*. The first task facing the founders of this new nation was to realize just that, in other words to "round out" Confederation.

Not only would the western areas have to be added to the new Dominion. Two of the Atlantic colonies — Prince Edward Island and Newfoundland — were still not part of the union in 1867; and in Nova Scotia, which had entered reluctantly, there was still a strong anti-Confederation feeling which would have to be changed.

Newfoundland's reasons for not wanting to join Confederation were made clear in a petition sent by merchants, traders, fishermen and other inhabitants of the island colony to the British government. It said in part :

2                                                    THE APPRENTICESHIP

The sentiments of all classes of (our) people have been, and still are, of the most loyal and devoted character. [Our necessities or demands for protection from the foreign enemy or from internal disturbance have never been a heavy burden or a serious cost to the Imperial Exchequer, while our most intimate commercial relations are held with Great Britain.

Newfoundland is practically more remote from the principal parts of Canada than from Britain itself, and has never had any political, and only minor commercial. connection with the former — a connection which is entirely cut off by the sea for nearly six months of the year, during which there can be no communication with Canada, except through the territories of a foreign power — the United States of America.]

The inhabitants of this colony would desire to see this island always retained separately by Britain, as its ocean fortress and military outpost in this part of the world, whatever might be the future destiny of the colonies of the mainland ... The colony has no community of interests with Upper or Lower Canada, and little with the other maritime provinces.

The Newfoundland merchants argued further that their entry into Confederation would only deprive them of what they called :

... those civil, constitutional and territorial rights which Newfoundland has so long held and so dearly prized; and for a loss so great there is no offer of substantial return.

The stubborn defiance of the Newfoundlanders was recognized as valid by the British authorities. However, Nova Scotia could make none of the same claims as the island of Newfoundland in order to stay out of Confederation, and because of its mainland location the Imperial Parliament considered Nova Scotia's participation essential.

Over the protests of the anti-Confederation forces who had begun their campaign in 1864, the British parliament, sure of its position, had refused to consider leaving Nova Scotia out of Confederation. So, as John A. Macdonald, the chief architect of Confederation, put it, Nova Scotia was "joined with the other colonies in Holy Matrimony". But no sooner had the marriage been consummated by the will of the British Parliament and the acquiescence of Queen Victoria, than Nova Scotia wanted a divorce.

The Nova Scotians made their displeasure known in the elections which followed Confederation, when they voted overwhelmingly in favour of anti-Confederation candidates. Of nineteen members sent to the new Parliament in Ottawa, only one (Sir Charles Tupper) had been a pro-Confederation candidate. The leader of Nova Scotia's fight against Confederation had been Joseph Howe, one of the most colorful personalities in Canadian history. When he lost the fight in his own province, and the Nova Scotia legislature agreed to send delegates to England for consultations with the Imperial government, Howe himself went to England, and for six months there he carried on a one-man campaign in an attempt to dissuade the British authorities from including Nova Scotia in the Confederation scheme. But to no avail. The imperial authorities were determined that Nova Scotia should become part of the Dominion of Canada, and it did.

Howe was elected one of the nineteen Nova Scotia members of the new Parliament in Ottawa, and he continued his fight in the very centre of the new Canadian state. In a letter to a newspaper he wrote :

[I, having expressed my determination to bow to the paramount authority of Parliament, and try the experiment, am not likely to be deterred ... from endeavouring to improve a measure which I believe to be sadly defective and to avert the evils wherewith it is charged.]

... It is said in other Canadian papers : "Howe has not repented of his opposition to Confederation". This is true. I have not repented, and never shall till the working of the measure falsifies my predictions. The page of my public life of whiich I shall ever be most justly proud is that whereon is unfolded the earnestness and sincerity with which, against fearful odds, I defended the independence of my native province, and endeavoured to protect her people from insult and spoliation ... [A new page is opening before us, on which is to be written the future of British America. Nova Scotia has one solemn obligation resting on her. It is to withdraw confidence which has been abused — to punish those by whom her settled convictions were disregarded and her franchises overriden.]

... A year hence, or five years hence, we may, if the advocates of this measure are not mistaken, have cause to rejoice; but just now, in Nova Scotia, we feel more like mourning. [Canada may exult because she has possessed herself of two noble provinces by intrigue, without cost of war. But] we have to mourn the loss of our independence, to fit a strange yoke upon our necks, to look at fisheries bargained away, staples without market, a Legislature shorn of all dignity and influence, and a future full of peril and uncertainty. [Oh no, you can hardly expect us to rejoice. There may come a time when the first of July may be a day of cheerfulness in Nova Scotia. This year, notwithstanding the zealous bluster of a few officials, it will be a day of gloom, of intense sorrow. And the fact that you have insultingly asked us to rejoice in our own degradation will but intensify the determination to punish those by whom we have been insulted and betrayed.

Upon reading such letters, and hearing his speeches, one observer commented :

It seemed as if another Samson were making ready to grasp with his mighty hands the pillars of our national fabric and overwhelm it in ruin.]

Howe returned to England to pursue his campaign in much the same manner as he had done before his province entered Confederation. Sir Charles Tupper, one of the Fathers of Confederation, whom the prime minister, John A. Macdonald, had assigned to the job of converting Howe, followed him. Tupper reported the following conversation — one of the most important in Canadian history.

HOWE : Well, I can't say that I am glad to see you, but we have to make the best of it.

TUPPER : I will not insult you by suggesting that you should fail to undertake the mission that brought you here. When you find out, however, that the Government and the Imperial Parliament are overwhelmingly against you, it is important for you to consider the next step.

HOWE : I have eight hundred men in each county in Nova Scotia who will take an oath that they will never pay a cent of taxation to the Dominion, and I defy the Government to enforce Confederation.

TUPPER : You have no power of taxation, Howe, and in a few years you will have every sensible man cursing you, as there will be no money for schools, roads or bridges. I will not ask that troops be sent to Nova Scotia, but I shall recommend that if the people refuse to obey the law that the Federal subsidy be withheld. You have a majority at your back, Howe, but I would remind you that all the judges, bishops and clergy, and the best element in your province have heartily supported the union. And if you enter the Cabinet and assist in carrying out the work of Confederation you will find me as strong a supporter as I have been an opponent.

Two hours of frank discussion followed, and that night Tupper was able to report to his prime minister that he thought Howe would enter the cabinet in Ottawa.

The battle was almost over. Howe returned immediately to Nova Scotia and advised against any further resistance. After many months of discussion it was arranged that special consideration would be given to Nova Scotia. The degree to which the Canadians were willing to go to accommodate Howe is indicated in the following letter which the prime minister wrote to him in January, 1869 :

> ...So anxious am I for the pacification of Nova Scotia, and so convinced that it can only be done through your patriotic exertions, that I am quite willing to depart from the usual constitutional course and to consult you as to the principle appointments in Nova Scotia, although you are not yet responsible for the advice you give...
>
> I have arranged with my colleagues to inform me of any vacancies in their several Departments, so that I can keep a roster of affairs and consult with you thereupon. The vacancy in the Senate should at once be filled up, and the choice should decidedly be from your own supporters. [Pray talk this matter over with Rose...]
>
> I look forward to having some fun about the judgeship to be vacated by Mr. Bliss. I think A. G. Archibald will have the first claim upon us here, and of his fitness there can be no doubt, both as to knowledge and respectability. I am glad to believe that you and he are on such terms now as to induce you to look upon the appointment with complacency.
>
> We shall want, whenever you are ready, a Railway commissioner. There are other offices which might be filled up, but which can stand over until things are further advanced.
>
> Believe me,
> My dear Howe,
> Yours sincerely,
> JOHN A. MACDONALD

After these important preliminaries, Howe became a member of the Canadian cabinet at the end of January, 1869 — a year and a half after Confederation became a fact. The battle was over. Nova Scotia had been pacified.

The Atlantic colonies of Prince Edward Island and Newfoundland still remained outside Confederation, but they would have to wait, for in the meantime new problems had arisen, not in the eastern part of the new Dominion, but in the territories to the west of it. Canada hoped to bring these territories into Confederation, but first it would have to pur-

chase them, for they belonged to the Hudson's Bay Company, and then acquire authority over them from the British government.

The purchase of the Northwest Territories proved easier to accomplish than the transfer of authority. In 1869 the Canadian government bought the Hudson's Bay Company lands for £ 300,000, and at the same time the British government agreed to the transfer of authority. The trouble started when the Canadians tried to put the transfer of authority into effect.

Ottawa appointed a Lieutenant-Governor in the person of William McDougall and sent him in haste to the Red River district of the Northwest Territories to establish a provisional government. This McDougall was never able to do, and his attempt caused an insurrection by the people living in this part of the west.

Most of the people of the Red River district, near the present city of Winnipeg, were called *Métis*. They were the descendents of the hired hands of the old North West Company, who had come to the west from Quebec in the early 19th century, and of the native Indians of the district.

In the 1820's there had been a struggle between the North West Company and the Hudson's Bay Company for authority over this vast domain, and the North West Company had used the Métis to protect its interests. It had encouraged them to claim large sections of the land in the name of their Indian mothers, and it was during this struggle that the Métis had enunciated for the first, but not for the last, time their identity as a corporate people, members of neither the Indian world nor the white man's world. They came to believe that they formed "une nation", a national entity with corporate rights.

By the time that Canada acquired the western lands from Hudson's Bay Company, in 1869, the Métis had begun to abandon their nomadic ways, and had settled down in rural communities, escaping a couple of times a year to participate in the buffalo hunt.

The Métis feared the advance of the white man into their territory. They feared contact with people from a more sophisticated society. And as French-speaking Roman Catholics they feared the advance of English-speaking Protestant settlers. In time, they felt, they would be so outnumbered that they would become an insignificant force in the west. As they saw it, they would lose their homes, their birthright, and their inheritance — *unless their corporate rights as a distinct and "in-between" people were granted by the new authority from Canada.*

This is what the insurrection of 1869 and '70 was all about. It was not a struggle to *prevent* the absorption of the Northwest Territories into Canada, but a struggle to *delay it until such time as the corporate rights of the Métis were granted.*

The leader and spokesman of the Métis was Louis Riel. He had gone east to Montreal for his education and returned to the Red River district shortly before the outbreak of the resistance movement there.

Four years after the insurrection was over, Riel wrote a report on the incident, in which he related the motives and actions of his followers.

> The Northwest Territories were transferred to Canada only on July 15, 1870. But the Canadian government had begun, in '68-'69, some public works in its own name in Rupert's Land in the North-West Territory, without the authorization of the Hudson's Bay Company. The arrival of the Canadian agents, in that country, was marked by the contempt they displayed for the authority of the company itself and for the old settlers. They sought to seize the best lands of the Métis, especially at Oak Point . . . 30 miles to the east of Fort Garry. They claimed to buy these lands from the Indians. And to strengthen themselves at the beginning of the struggle against us, they sought to form an alliance with the Indians, and to get them on their side sold them intoxicating liquors contrary to the law! Besides, the superintendent of the Canadian works at Oak Point, Mr. Snow, and also his subordinates conducted themselves very badly : on one occasion they came near murdering one another . . . One can imagine that in acting in this fashion these strangers gave the settlers an impression of themselves which was not at all favourable. [The authorities of the Hudson's Bay Company were obliged to take severe measures against these disorders. But they protested to the Canadian government less because of

the bad conduct of its employees than for their having undertaken, without authority, public works on their territory.]

After Mr. Snow had begun the work on the Dawson Road between the Lake of the Woods and Oak Point in '68, in the name of Canada, another intruder from the same country had in the summer of '69 also begun to survey around Fort Garry public and private lands, according to a new system of survey, upsetting without any explanation whatsoever the settled order of things, and troubling without compunction the old settlers in the peaceful and legal possession of their lands.

The protests of the government of the Hudson's Bay Company were soon followed by those of the settlers who opposed themselves resolutely to the fact that men as suspect as these should in so unwarranted a fashion open public roads and lay out surveys on their lands, in the name of a foreign government.

It was at the time of these incidents that the first Lieutenant-Governor of the new territories, William McDougall, arrived at the border with instructions to prepare for the official transfer by appointing a Legislative Council. He brought with him three councillors-designate and, according to Riel, a considerable consignment of rifles. Riel related that :

The alarmed Métis organized themselves "in a national committee" and went to meet Mr. McDougall, sending him some messengers to tell him specifically not to enter their country in that fashion. Mr. Dougall made an insulting and disdainful reply. Many hangers-on of Mr. Snow... had already declared that they had come from Ontario in advance of Mr. McDougall, as a military force, being fully decided to impose Mr. McDougall on us as governor, by strong-arm methods if necessary...

The Métis people claimed that they had never been officially informed by England or by the Hudson's Bay Company about the transfer of authority. They sent an order to McDougall, adjoining him not to enter the colony, and on November 2, 1869 the Métis occupied Fort Garry, the most important post and the seat of the territorial government of the Hudson's Bay Company.

Fourteen days later, W. Mactavish, of the Hudson's Bay Company, governor of the territory, issued a proclamation to inhabitants in which he deplored what he called the "unlawful actions" of the Métis in seizing Fort Garry and in holding public meetings. [He concluded by saying...

Therefore, in the interests of Law and order, in behalf of all the securities you have for life and property, and in a word for the sake of the present and the future welfare of the Settlement and its inhabitants, I *again earnestly and emphatically PROTEST against each and all of those unlawful acts and intents.*

I charge those engaged in them, before they are irretrievably and hopelessly involved, immediately to disperse themselves, and peaceably to depart to their habitations, or to their lawful business, under the pains and penalties of law ...

You are dealing with a crisis out of which may come incalculable good or immeasurable evil, and with all the weight of my official authority, and all the influence of my individual position, let me finally charge you to adopt only such means as are lawful and constitutional, rational and safe.

Given under my hand and seal at Fort Garry this sixteenth day of November, 1869 ...]

Riel disregarded the proclamation and called a meeting of the National Committee of the Métis to agree on the measures to be taken to further their cause. Riel related :

The National Committee of the Métis took its precautions in order that our public affairs should not, by a piece of trickery, fall into the hands of a sham Lieutenant-Governor from Canada ... On November 24 the Committee, wishing to protect the public accounts and funds from the plot that the friends of Mr. McDougall were weaving, put a strong guard around the books and funds in question.

Meanwhile McDougall was becoming more and more dissatisfied. On Nov. 17, 1869, he had received a letter from certain individuals in Winnipeg, inviting him to take immediate possession of the territory, and on December 1 he proclaimed the annexation of Rupert's Land and of the Northwest to Canada.

The Métis responded by jailing some of the Canadians, and one week after McDougall's proclamation of annexation Riel proclaimed the formation of a Provisional Government of his own. He commented :

Because of the circumstances which had given rise to it that government was legal.

In the face of these new developments, the Canadian government sent emissaries to the North West to deal with Riel and his followers. On January 19, 1870, a general meeting of the inhabitants heard the assurances of the emissaries that the North West would be fairly and equally treated within Confederation. A week later forty delegates met in a convention at the courthouse in Fort Garry. During the convention three delegates were sent to Ottawa to further the cause of the Métis. The wishes of the Métis were embodied in a List of Rights which stated, in part :

> ... That the Territories heretofore known as Rupert's Land and the North-West shall not enter into the Confederation of the Dominion of Canada except as a Province... and with all the rights and privileges common to the different Provinces of the Dominion.
> ... That the schools be separate, and that the public money for schools be distributed among the different religious denominations in proportion to their respective populations according to the system in the province of Quebec.
> ... That the English and French languages be common in the Legislature and in the courts, and that all public documents as well as all acts of the Legislature be published in both languages. [... That all debts contracted by the Provisional Government of the Territory of the North-West... in consequence of the illegal and inconsiderate measures adopted by Canadian officials to bring about a civil war in our midst, be paid out of the Dominion Treasury.]

While the three Métis envoys were in Ottawa stating their terms, there occurred in the North West the event which marked the turning point in the whole North West affair : Louis Riel had one of the Canadians, an Ontario Orangeman, Thomas Scott, executed by a firing squad at Fort Garry.

Riel claimed that Scott had been the cause of the insubordination shown by the Canadian prisoners taken by the Métis, and that an example had to be shown before the Métis guards retaliated and a general massacre ensued.

One leading Canadian historian has said that the execution of Scott "looms as the most determinative specific political incident between Confederation and the Great War",* for it led to other clashes between French and English, Catholic and Protestant, thus digging up the hatchet that was supposed

---

* A. R. M. Lower : *Colony to Nation.*

to have been buried at the time of Confederation and opening once again a gulf between the two linguistic groups of Canada.

Things moved quickly following the death of Scott, and in 1870 the Canadian government passed the Manitoba Act which created the province of Manitoba, and which granted most of the demands which the Métis had made in their Lists of Rights. An expeditionary force was sent to the new province to restore order and effect the transfer of authority. In the first federal election held in Manitoba Riel was elected to be sent to Ottawa, but he was never permitted to take his seat. The province of Ontario had offered $5,000 for his capture following the execution of Scott, and after being sworn in in Ottawa, Riel escaped to Quebec, and thence to the United States.

Agitation over the question of amnesty to those who had participated in the resistance continued for five years. Ontario insisted that it should not include Riel and other leaders who had had anything to do with Scott's death, while Quebec insisted that it should. The matter was finally resolved by banishing the leaders. Yet Riel was not to be forgotten, not by his Métis people, nor the French-Canadians, nor the Ontarians.

Riel would return into Canadian history and the cry of his people, uttered for the first time in 1870, would be heard again in the not-too-distant future :

> We *may* be a small community, and a half-breed community at that — but we are men, free and spirited men, and we will not allow even the Dominion of Canada to trample on our rights...

While all these events were taking place in what is now Manitoba, in the British colonies beyond the Rocky Mountains a momentous decision was about to be made. In 1849 a British colony called Vancouver Island had been established and the Hudson's Bay Company had been given a title deed to the colony, provided the company could promote settlement. But they were not very successful; nor did they meet with much more success in the mainland region which is now British Columbia.

Then in 1858 gold was discovered on the Fraser River. Hundreds of people poured into the colony, and when, four years later, more strikes were made in the Cariboo region, hundreds more came from the United States. The influx of settlers made it necessary for the mainland to become a separate colony in order to supervise the construction of various public works which would permit the efficient exploitation of the gold. But by 1866 the gold was gone and the colony was saddled with an immense public debt. The colony of Vancouver Island was then united to the colony on the mainland to form the province of British Columbia. The British Columbians wondered what to do with themselves. The gold rush was over, but life had to go on.

Should British Columbia continue eternally as a dependent colony of Great Britain, isolated at the far end of the continent? Nobody was in favour of this. Should it annex itself to the United States? Many of the merchants favoured this. Or should it join the Canadian Confederation? This appealed to many of the British settlers, but being tied to a country thousands of miles away had obvious drawbacks. It is not surprising, therefore, that when the British Columbian representatives met with the Canadian government one of the most important terms of the proposed union was to be a railway linking the Pacific province with the rest of the Dominion. In 1871 an act was passed, allowing for the entry of British Columbia into Confederation. Article 11 of that act read as follows:

> The Government of the Dominion undertake to secure the commencement simultaneously, within two years from the date of the Union, of the construction of a Railway from the Pacific towards the Rocky Mountains, and from such points as may be selected, east of the Rocky Mountains towards the Pacific, to connect the seabord of British Columbia with the railway system of Canada; and further, to secure the completion of such Railway within ten years from the date of the union...

A gigantic undertaking — a railway almost 3,000 miles long, passing over rough terrain and through unpopulated regions.

The comparison may seem almost comical, but it was also the need for a railway — or for money to complete a railway —

that finally led to the entry of another province into Confederation two years later : Prince Edward Island on the other end of the continent.

It is ironic that tiny Prince Edward Island had remained outside of Confederation, for it was here that the first pre-Confederation conference had taken place, in 1864. From time to time after 1867 the Canadian government had made overtures to the little Atlantic colony, but its absence from the union was not considered a serious matter.

But in 1871 the Islanders decided to treat themselves to the luxury of a three-million-dollar railway, and building began immediately. "It was on this railway", writes a recent Island historian, "that the Island rode into Confederation."* For when the Islanders found themselves on the verge of bankruptcy as a result of the new venture, union with the mainland did not seem so bad after all.

So early in 1873 delegates from the Island arrived in Ottawa to make financial arrangements with the Canadian government, and on July 1st of that year — the sixth anniversary of Confederation — Prince Edward Island — where Confederation had been born — became Canada's sixth province.

The other island colony, Newfoundland, still remained outside confederation. It would not be until the middle of the 20th century that Joseph E. Smallwood would lead his Newfoundland people into the Canadian Confederation.

Nevertheless, by 1873 Canada did have a Dominion from Sea to Sea.

---

* Lorne C. Callbeck : "The Cradle of Confederation", p. 223.

# A LINK OF STEEL                    2
## *The CPR and the "Pacific Scandal"*

When Canada's founding fathers were making their plans for
the union of Britain's North American colonies into the
Dominion of Canada, they all stressed the importance of a railway linking the colonies. In 1865 Alexander Galt, the financial
wizard of Confederation, said that up until then :

> Intercolonial trade has been of the most insignificant character.
> We have looked far more to our commercial relations with the
> neighbouring country than to the interchange of our own products.

Galt then gave examples of the interchange of products which
a union of the British colonies would make possible.

> ... We may hope to supply Newfoundland and the great fishing
> districts of the Gulf with the agricultural products of Western
> Canada. We may hope to obtain from Nova Scotia our supply of
> coal. And the manufacturing industry of Lower Canada may hope
> to find more extensive outlets in supplying many of those articles
> which are now purchased in foreign markets.

All of the Fathers of Confederation agreed that the British
colonies in North America had to become more *interdependent*

if they were to become more *independent* of the United States. An intercolonial railway was a prerequisite to this.

By the time Manitoba and British Columbia had entered Confederation, four years after its initiation, an intercolonial railway had become a pressing necessity. It was, in fact, one of the terms under which the two provinces agreed to join the union.

So the Canadian government was going to finance a railway from the Atlantic Ocean right across the country to its newest province on the Pacific Ocean. But who was going to build it ? Two groups turned out to be interested. One of these was headed by Sir Hugh Allan, a Scottish-born Montreal ship-owner and Canada's richest man, and the other by a Toronto financier, David Lewis MacPherson.

The prime minister, Sir John A. Macdonald, was in a quandary. Sir Hugh Allan was the senior of the two rivals, but many in his syndicate represented American interests, and Sir John was determined that this should be a Canadian railway. Mac-Pherson, on the other hand, was known to be a personal friend of Macdonald.

Macdonald decided that no charter could be given to any company in 1871. The elections of 1872 were about to take place, and Macdonald was determined to arrange the amalga-mation of the two groups before the government met again after the elections. He wanted the Americans on Sir Hugh Allan's group to be replaced by Torontonians from Mac-Pherson's group. However, neither group wanted to amalgamate with the other. And Sir Hugh Allan was still determined to be president of the company which would build the railway, and to have controlling interests for himself, which he could then distribute to his American partners. At least, this inter-pretation seems to be suggested by the following letter which Allan wrote to one of his American friends :

> Dear Mr. McMullen :— I have been hoping from day to day that some conclusion which I could communicate to you would be arrived at, respecting the Pacific Railroad negotiations, but some obstacle to cause delay always intervened. The near approach of

the elections, however, ... has at length brought the matter to a crisis, and I think the game I have been playing is now likely to be attended with success.

Yesterday we entered into an agreement, by which the Government bound itself to form a company of Canadians only, according to my wishes. That the company will make me President, and that I and my friends will get a majority of the stock, and that the contract for building the road will be given to this company, in terms of the Act of Parliament. Americans are to be carefully excluded ... But I fancy we can get over that some way or other.

This position has not been attained without large payments of money. I have already paid over $200,000 and I will have at least $100,000 more to pay ...

Yours truly,

Hugh Allan

In an earlier letter to another of his American friends, Sir Hugh Allan had explained how he had managed to force the government's hand — by seeking out its most vulnerable point. He found it in George Etienne Cartier, Macdonald's French-Canadian colleague. Cartier's position as leader of French Canada was in serious jeopardy. The organization he had spent years building had passed into the hands of aggressive and ambitious young men who were beginning to tire of the old man's ways. Allan understood very well that Macdonald's strength depended on Cartier's strength in Quebec, and in his letter Allan wrote :

"The French party ... has sustained and kept in office and existence the entire Government for the last five years. It consists of 45 men who have followed Cartier and voted in a solid phalanx for all his measures. The Government majority in Parliament being generally less than 45 it follows that the defection of one half or two thirds would at any time put the government out of office. It was therefore evident that some means must be adopted to bring the influence of this compact body of members to bear in our favour, and as soon as I had made up my mind what was the best course to pursue, I did not lose a moment in following it up.

A railroad from Montreal to Ottawa, through the French country, north of the Ottawa River, has long been desired by the French inhabitants; but Cartier, who is the salaried solicitor of the Grand Trunk Road, to which this would be an opposition, has interposed difficulties, and by his influence prevented its being built. The same reason made him desirous of giving the contract for the Canada Pacific into the hands of parties connected with the Grand

Trunk Railway, and to this end he fanned the flame of opposition to us. But I saw in this French railroad scheme and in the near approach of the general elections, when Cartier will have to go to his constituents for re-election, a sure means of obtaining my object ...

I employed several young French lawyers to write it up for their own newspapers. I subscribed a controlling interest in the stock, and proceeded to subsidize the newspapers themselves, both editors and proprietors. I went to the country through which the road would pass, and called on many of the inhabitants. I visited the priests, and made friends of them, and I employed agents to go among the principal people and talk it up. I then began to hold public meetings, and attended to them myself, making frequent speeches in French to them, showing them where their true interest lay. The scheme at once became popular, and I formed a committee to influence the members of the Legislature. This succeeded so well that, in a short time, I had 27 out of 45 on whom I could rely, and the electors of the ward in this city, which Cartier himself represents, notified him that unless the contract for the Pacific Railway were given in the interests of Lower Canada, he need not present himself for re-election.

... He then agreed to give the contract, as required, in a way that there would be 17 provisional directors, of which Ontario would have eight, and we nine, thereby giving us the control. We at once proceeded to organize the company, and they named me President ... and we have notified the government that we are willing to take the contract for building the Canada Pacific Railway ...

In the same letter Sir Hugh Allan explained how he managed to make the American company appear to be a Canadian one.

... The next thing to be done is to subscribe stock, which must be done by British subjects only ... I have arranged ... that if you will send a certificate of the equivalent of $1,000,000 gold, having been placed by Jay Cooke & Co. to the credit of the Merchants' Bank of Canada, Montreal, in their own bank in New York, it will accept the cheques for subscription, but no money will pass till the contract is entered into, and then ten percent of the whole amount of stock awarded us will have to be paid into the Receiver General. Be pleased, therefore, to send me as early as possible, powers of attorney to subscribe stock, and Jay Cooke & Co's certificate above mentioned. I have had several letters from England, offering to take the whole thing up if we desire to part with it, but it looks to me to be too good to part with readily.

... As you may suppose, the matter has not reached this point without great expense ... I think it will reach not much short of $300,000.

Yours faithfully,

Hugh Allan.

Astute businessman that he was, Sir Hugh had estimated the amount exactly. After the election of 1872, it was found that he poured close to $300,000 into the Conservative party during the election campaign.

It was indeed a most unsatisfactory arrangement. Sir John A. Macdonald's party, which continued to form the government after the 1872 elections, was indebted to the tune of $300,000 to someone with whom it was to do the most important business of the nation — a business which would involve thousands of acres of land, and millions of dollars in subsidies and various other protective arrangements.

It was, of course, impossible that all this should remain secret, and before Parliament met again after the elections, the Liberal member for Shefford, Quebec, L.S. Huntingdon, obtained evidence of this "deal" between the government and Allan's syndicate. On April 2, 1873, in the House of Commons Huntingdon made a motion for a special inquiry, alleging :

> That in anticipation of the Legislation of last Session as to the Pacific Railway, an agreement was made between Sir Hugh Allan acting for himself and certain other Canadian Promoters, and G. W. McMullen, acting for certain United States Capitalists, whereby the latter agreed to furnish all the funds necessary for the construction of the contemplated Railway, and to give the former a certain percentage of interest in consideration of their interest and position, the scheme agreed upon being ostensibly that of a Canadian Company with Sir Hugh Allan at its head, —
> That the Government were aware that these negotiations were pending between the said parties, —
> That subsequently an understanding was come to between the Government, Sir Hugh Allan and Mr. Abbott, [one of the Members of the Honourable House of Commons of Canada,] that Sir Hugh Allan and his friends should advance a large sum of money for the purpose of aiding the elections of Ministers and their supporters at the ensuing general elections, and that he and his friends should receive the contract for the construction of the Railway, —
> That accordingly Sir Hugh Allan did advance a large sum of money for the purpose mentioned, and at the solicitation and under the pressing instances of Ministers, —
> That part of the moneys expended by Sir Hugh Allan in connection with the obtaining of the Act of Incorporation and Charter, were paid to him by the said United States Capitalists under the agreement with him...

The public, of course, demanded that these charges be proved or disproved. Some people feared that the government would just prorogue the House while a Royal Commission sat investigating the charges. The Liberals, and even some influential Conservatives, wanted the charges to be investigated by a special committee of Parliament, where members of the government would have to answer the charges against them. At a special meeting, called to prevent the Government from proroguing Parliament, L.S. Huntingdon, who had uncovered the scandal, asked :

> When Sir John A. Macdonald called himself a man, and when, laying his hand on his heart, he declared that there was no truth whatever in the charges which had been made, was it likely he would have appeared before the committee and have said that there were papers in the hands of another party which would prove all charges against him, and which he had sought to destroy? (Cheers) Was it likely that he would have told them of that telegram asking for another $10,000 with the assurance that he would, if he got that last demand, ask for no more? (Cheers)

At the same meeting Edward Blake, a leading Liberal, gave his reasons for wanting an open parliamentary investigation of the charges against the government :

> Among the members, every man may not be as deeply dyed in this iniquity as the Ministry; some may not have known that they added to the crime of corrupting constituencies that of selling their country. But those who did know will resist investigation to the last, as their crime is only a little less than those who perpetrated it.

A parliamentary Commission of Inquiry was appointed, and after it had heard all the evidence, but before it had made its report, the Governor-General, the Earl of Dufferin, wrote to the prime minister as follows :

> My Dear Sir John,
> It is with greater pain than ever I did anything in my life that I now sit down to write to you, but I feel it is but justice you should know the conclusions to which I fear I am being forced by a most anxious study of the evidence adduced before the Commission. Of course, until an authoritative copy of that evidence is placed in my hands, I am not required to arrive at a decision; it is not, therefore, as the Governor-General of Canada that I address you, but as a warm and sincere friend desirous of putting you on your guard against eventualities which it is well you should provide against in time. I am the more anxious to do this, as the friendly spirit I have evinced towards you during the course of this unfortunate business may have led you to count upon my support, beyond the point to which I might find myself able to extend it.

But however deeply I may sympathise with you in your difficulties — difficulties into which you have been drawn in a great measure by circumstances beyond your control — I shall be bound to sacrifice my personal inclinations to what may become my duty to my Sovereign and this country.

What I feel is simply this — [that although it has been distinctly proved that in numerous respects you have been the victim of the most atrocious calumnies — that your personal honour is as stainless as it has ever been — that in spite of many inducements to the contrary, in spite of Cartier's weakness, you have religiously protected the interests of Canada, both against American speculators who addressed you, and against the approaches of Sir Hugh Allan —] that although it has evidently never entered into your thoughts to make a single illegitimate concession in consideration of the support and assistance you expected on other grounds to receive from Allan — it is still an indisputable and patent fact that you and some of your colleagues have been the channels through which extravagant sums of money — derived from a person with whom you were negotiating on the part of the Dominion — were distributed throughout the constituencies of Ontario and Quebec, and have been applied to purposes forbidden by the statutes.

This circumstance carries with it the further ill effect of rendering the arbitrament of Parliament itself untrustworthy.

In acting as you have, I am well convinced that you have only followed a traditional practice, and that probably your political opponents have resorted with equal freedom to the same expedients, but as Minister of Justice and the official guardian and protector of the laws, your responsibilities are exceptional and your immediate and personal connection with what has occurred cannot but fatally affect your position as a Minister.

I need not say what distress I experience in making this communication to you. Independent of the personal attachment I feel toward you, I have always had, and still have the greatest faith and confidence in your ability, patriotism, integrity and statesmanship. I believe there is no one in the country capable of administering its affairs to greater advantage than yourself.

It is to you, in fact, that Canada owes its existence, and your name will be preserved in History as the Father and Founder of the Dominion. But no considerations of this kind are sufficient, I fear, to affect the present situation, controlled, as it is, by a special and immediate necessity.

This letter ... as I said before, is not an announcement, but a friendly confidence in respect of a future contingency that I now make to you ... I do not even say that the conclusions I have thus shadowed forth, are actually formed within my mind, but I feel it is but fair to let you know the tendency of my thoughts at the present moment.

Yours sincerely,

Dufferin.

Following the commission's report, a vote of censure in Parliament brought the fall of the government of Sir John A. Macdonald, Canada's first prime minister. The Liberals' Alexander Mackenzie took over the government, and, in 1874, while the Pacific scandal was still fresh in the minds of the public, he called an election. The voters confirmed the Liberals' position, giving them an overwhelming majority. Mackenzie's government was to remain in power for the next four years. It was during this period that the western part of the Pacific Railway was begun, but a world-wide depression which had begun in 1873 dried up Canadian sources of money in the London market, and made it impossible for the Liberal government to pursue the railway project wholeheartedly. British Columbia, which had entered Confederation on the understanding that it would be linked to the rest of Canada by rail, was threatening secession. When the Liberal government's four-year term expired, the electors brought back Sir John A. Macdonald's Conservatives in the election of 1878. Macdonald was determined to continue the building of the Pacific Railway — but not as a public project.

By 1880 the availability of foreign capital had increased, and a private company was given the contract to build the entire road. But the new company did not assume all the risk. Its agreement with the government read, in part :

> ... Upon the organization of the said company, and the deposit by them, with the Government, of one million dollars ..., and in consideration of the completion and perpetual and efficient operation of the railway by the said Company, the Government may grant to the Company a subsidy of twenty-five million dollars in money and twenty-five million acres of land ... and may also grant to the Company the land for right of way, stations, and other purposes, and such other privileges as are provided for in the said contract.

The contract also included a famous monopoly clause, which forbade the construction of any competing railway line to the south of the CPR line for a period of twenty years. The syndicate which signed this agreement with the government was headed by George Stephen, president of the Bank of Montreal. Charles Tupper, who introduced the government's new railway legislation, concluded his now famous address with the following declaration of hope :

> ... Under the proposals now submitted for Parliament to consider, this country is going to secure the construction and operation of the gigantic work which is to give new life and vitality to every section of this Dominion. No greater responsibility rests upon any body of men in this Dominion, than rests upon the Government of Canada, placed as it is in a position to deal with the enormous work of the development of such a country as Providence has given us; and I say we should be traitors to ourselves and to our children if we should hesitate to secure on terms such as we have the pleasure of submitting to Parliament the construction of this work, which is going to develop all the enormous resources of the North-West, and to pour into that country a tide of population which will be a tower of strength to every part of Canada, a tide of industrious and intelligent men who will not only produce national as well as individual wealth in that section of the Dominion, but will create such a demand for the supplies which must come from the older provinces, as will give new life and vitality to every industry in which those provinces are engaged.

But the Liberal opposition was not impressed. They considered the building of an all-Canadian railway a monstruous folly of nationalism. They insisted that the railway should pass into the United States instead of going through the unprofitable and infertile lands of Canada, north of Lake Superior.

The Liberals also protested the generous subsidies the government agreed to provide to the private company, and brought into being a rival company which they said could build the railway much more cheaply. In spite of the Liberals' protests, Macdonald's government was able to proceed with its own plan, thanks to its majority in Parliament.

But the construction of the Canadian Pacific Railway was not clear sailing even after these initial hurdles had been passed.

Both the Grand Trunk Railway and the Hudson's Bay Company considered the Canadian Pacific to be a rival intruding into their trade territories, and they proceeded to make it impossible for the new syndicate to obtain money to continue with the building of the railway. So well did the Grand Trunk Railway and the Hudson's Bay Company do their work with the financial houses of Great Britain, that within two years after the signing of the original contract the Canadian Pacific Company found itself unable to sell its stock or land, grant bonds, or to obtain in any other way the money needed for the railway.

By the end of 1883, the company was in a desperate financial situation, and had to appeal to the government for a loan of $22,500,000. George Stephen, president of the company, was on the verge of giving up, and he wrote to the prime minister :

> My Dear Sir John :
>
> ... You may be sure I will do all I can to keep things moving, and in life, till relief arrives, but you must not blame me if I fail. I do not, at the moment, see how we are to get the money to keep the work going, but I will know better what I can do when I get to Montreal, and consult with my colleagues.
>
> If I find we cannot go on, I suppose the only thing to do will be to put in a Receiver; if that has to be done, the quicker it is done the better. Of course I will do nothing without first seeing you. I am getting so wearied and worn out with this business that almost any change will be a relief to me. Whatever happens, I shall always feel grateful for the readiness which you have throughout shown to help us in every possible way.
>
> Always yours,
>
> George Stephen.

The government made the loan, but all through the summer and fall of 1884 the company continued to be in serious financial trouble. In December the workmen went on strike because there was no money to pay them. Stephen and his colleague Donald Smith borrowed first $650,000, and later another million dollars, for which they had to give their personal guarantees.

Then in March 1885 the Indians and half-breeds of the Northwest Territories — the area west of the province of Manitoba — rose up against the Canadian government in protest against its unfair treatment of the Indians and its system of land tenure. The Canadian government was able to dispatch troops to the Northwest quickly and efficiently — thanks to the new railway, which fortunately had been completed that far west. Fifteen years earlier there had been a rebellion in the Northwest and it had taken troops two months to make the trip from Ottawa.

This time it took six days. This was a spectacular demonstration of the value of the railway; Parliament was duly impressed, and two months later it arranged for a five million dollar loan which it had previously refused. [William Van Horne, general manager of the Canadian Pacific Company, once proposed that the company should erect a monument to the memory of Louis Riel — leader of the Northwest rebellion.] Further loans followed, and shortly afterwards Barings of London announced that they would lend £3,000,000 sterling to the company. With private capital again available, the main financial hurdle had been crossed.

The physical obstacles proved to be just as difficult as the financial ones. Construction difficulties were greater than had been expected. The mere transportation of supplies to the railway sites was an enormous problem, especially during the winter. The vast prairie section was the easiest. The most difficult were the rocky, marshy and inaccessible stretch north of Lake Superior and the stretch through the western mountains, linking the completed sections on both sides.

To join the two completed sections of the railroad, the Canadian Pacific had to cross two ranges of mountains. Through the Rockies a satisfactory pass — the Kicking Horse Pass — was found. However, on the other side of the Rockies lay the great rounded slopes of the Selkirk Mountains. It was not until the summer of 1882 that the Rogers Pass was discovered.

If George Stephen, with his background as a bank president, deserves credit for seeing the Canadian Pacific Railway through its first financial crises, it was an American, William Cornelius Van Horne, with his background as general superintendent of several American railways, who deserves credit for solving the practical problems of construction involved in finishing the Canadian Pacific in record time.

A characteristic story is told of Van Horne's determination to get on with the job. He called one of his engineers to his office and, pointing to a map said :

Some infernal idiot has put a tunnel in there !

He asked how long it would take to build, and when the engineer suggested a year to 18 months, the general manager roared :

> What are they thinking about ? Are we going to hold up this railway for a year and a half while they build their damn tunnel ? Take it out.

The last spike of the Canadian Pacific Railway was driven by Donald Smith at Craigellachie, British Columbia, on November 7, 1885. Fifteen years after the project had begun, John A. Macdonald saw his dream of a transcontinental railway become a reality. During those fifteen years the Pacific scandal had temporarily wrecked Sir John's political career. And even when he had returned to public favour — and to power, his dream was always clouded by the threat of imminent financial disaster.

Now the railway was an accomplished fact. Sir John's Dominion from sea to sea was linked by a road of steel.

# "THOSE MY CLAIMS" 3
## The Northwest Rebellion of 1885

On July 20, 1885, in a courtroom in Regina, in what is now Saskatchewan, but was then the Northwest Territories, Louis David Riel was charged on oath that he :

> ... did maliciously and traitorously attempt and endeavour by force and arms to subvert and destroy the Constitution and Government of this realm as by law established.

This was the climax of an agitation which had begun some fifteen years earlier and which had taken, as the years went on, a form of constitutional agitation. It was only when the Métis, or half-breeds, of the North West Territories and the Indians of the same territory were exasperated at the injustice of their treatment, and it was only when they realized, in the words of Prime Minister Wilfrid Laurier, that

> the government instead of remedying their grievances sent a police force in order to overawe the people;

it was only then that the agitation developed into an open rebellion. The reasons for this rebellion can be best seen in the light of the participating groups : the Indians and the Métis. What did either want ? What did either complain about ? What was it that exasperated them so that the Indians took to the warpath and the Métis defied the legitimate government of their country ?

First, the Indians. There is no doubt that they constituted the gravest and most serious problem which faced the Canadian government in the maintenance of its sovereignty and authority in the North West. Following the usual pattern of those days, the Government negotiated special treaties with the Indians and set aside reserves for their use.

A typical treaty with the Indians would begin with a statement, as in the following treaty with the Blood Indians and other tribes of the region south of Calgary, relinquishing their claims :

> Whereas the said commissioners [of the Canadian Government] have proceeded to negotiate a treaty with the said Indians; and the same has been finally agreed upon and concluded [as follows, that is to say] : the Blackfeet, Blood, Piegan, Sarcee, Stony and other Indians inhabiting the district . . . do hereby cede, release, surrender, and yield up to the Government of Canada for Her Majesty the Queen and her successors forever, all their rights, titles and privileges whatsoever to the lands included within the following limits . . . (etc.)

In return for yielding these, their lands; in return for the concession of one square mile per Indian family of five; in return for the pleasure of living within the confines of reserves for what appeared to be eternity; in return for 12 dollars in cash to each man, woman and child of the various Indian families (and this as a token of Her Majesty's appreciation of their good behaviour); in return for an annual grant of 25 dollars to each chief, 15 dollars to each minor chief or councillor, and five dollars to every other Indian of whatever age; in return for an annual subsidy of $2,000 toward the purchase of ammunition; in return for a suit to each chief, minor chief and councillor; in return for a suitable medal or flag and for a Winchester rifle, ten axes, five handsaws, five augers, one grindstone and the necessary files and whetstones; in return for a maximum of 4 cows, one bull, two hoes, one spade, one scythe, and two hay forks, one plough and one harrow for every three families; in return for enough potatoes for each band, and for barley, oats and wheat; and in return for such teachers as the Canadian government would see fit to send when the Indians would "desire" them; in return for all this bounty, the Indians :

> ... do hereby solemnly promise and engage to strictly observe this treaty, and also to conduct and behave themselves as good and loyal subjects of Her Majesty the Queen. They promise and engage that they will, in all respects, obey and abide by the law, that they will maintain peace and good order between each other, [and other tribes of Indians and between themselves] and others of Her Majesty's subjects, whether Indians, Half-breeds, or whites, now inhabiting, or hereafter to inhabit, any part of the said ceded tract; and that they will not molest the person or property of any inhabitant of such ceded tract, or the property of Her Majesty the Queen, or interfere with or trouble any person passing or travelling through the said tract or any part thereof, and that they will assist the officers of Her Majesty in bringing to justice and punishment any Indian offending against the stipulations of this treaty, or infringing the laws in force in the country so ceded.

This cozy document did not in the least suggest how the Indians were to be helped in meeting the onslaught of the white man's civilization. It is a sad record; for it is the record of a people who found it impossible to adapt themselves to new and sometimes reprehensible practices in trade, to alcoholic spirits, and to the disappearance of their sole means of livelihood : the hunt. The buffalo disappeared rapidly as the population of settlers increased. The disappearance of the buffalo was a severe blow to the economic independence of the Indians. Even more tragic than this, however, was the fact that the Indian's land was taken away from him by land speculators and traders who defied both the Government and the Indians. The contempt of the white man for the Indians increased as fanatics entered the territories. It may safely be said that the Indians never understood the treaties. They perhaps understood the form, but the meaning and consequences of these treaties were totally lost to them. This is certainly what the Indians implied when at a meeting in 1884, they said in part :

> The Indian was blind in regard to making the treaty. He understood not the treaty when he heard of it. He did not see what use he had for it. He was then rich... The country was free to him wherever he wanted to go.

By the terms of the treaty he was shoved aside onto reserves. The Catholic Archibishop of St. Boniface, Alexandre Taché, who had spent his adult life in the territories, once discussed the grave psychological implications inherent in the limiting of the movement of the Indians :

> Never will Canada know and fully realize what hardship she has caused the Indians in parking them on reserves where they suffered the pains of hunger and pondered over their semi-captivity. The result of this decision has been that today the Indian has been dehumanized, his dignity has been shattered, his independence destroyed; and every day he battles hunger and the vices and disgusting practices of the white man. One must have seen this degeneration to understand the extent of the sufferings of the Indian people.

Nobody seems to have asked the simple question : what were the Indians to do on their wretched reserves ? As they could no longer hunt the buffalo, agriculture was their only way out. But a nomadic people cannot be changed overnight into an agricultural people. And then, as if the processes of change and adaptation were not difficult enough, a severe economic depression occurred in the territories in 1883 and 1884. The failure of crops meant famine. The Canadian government, suffering also from the financial impact of the depression, decided to curtail its expenses and so proceeded to lower the subsidies granted to the Indians. Superintendent Crozier of the North West Mounted Police warned against the Government's senseless policy in a letter to the Minister of Interior dated June 25, 1884 :

> Considering all that is at stake, it is poor, yes, false, economy to cut down the expenditure so closely in connection with the feeding of the Indians. Do not be too economical at once, for such a policy will be far the most expensive in the end. My firm conviction is, if some such policy as I have outlined is not carried out, there is only one other and that is to fight them.

The great missionary Bishop Grondin, once related that an Indian chief asked him with tears streaming down his face :

> What are we to become ? I do not fear for myself. I am old and will soon be dead. But I see no hope for my children and the children of my children. The whites tell us to work — but what can we do if no one helps us ? On our own we cannot even make a garden the size of one of our tents.

The climax of Indian agitation was reached on July 31, 1884. All the most important chiefs and a great number of Indians attended a meeting at which Big Bear declared :

> I have been trying to seize the promises which they made to me; I have been grasping but I cannot find them. What they have promised me straightway I have not yet the half of it. They have given me to choose between several small reserves but I feel sad to abandon the liberty of my own land.

In the face of mounting criticisms from the Indians, missionaries, and their own administrators out west, the Government appointed a special commissioner to investigate. His report proved to be short-sighted and an almost complete whitewash of the Government's action. Unable to obtain redress from the authorities, the Indians made preparations for their 1885 council. However there was no Indian council in 1885, but a rebellion. In the face of what the Leader of the Opposition in Ottawa called :

> ... neglects, delays, incompetence, bad appointments, mistaken policies, and breach of promises ...

the Indians fulfilled Superintendent Crozier's view that ...

> ... if some such policy as I have outlined is not carried out, there is only one other, and that is to fight them.

What now of the Métis, or half breed ? When the Canadian government obtained possession of the lands of the Hudson's Bay Company, it obtained at the same time jurisdiction over a people who were to play a great role in the development of the West — the half-breed Métis. The Manitoba Act of 1870 which created the province of Manitoba had unfortunate effects on the population who inhabited the Red River region. It brought about an economic revolution, for newcomers sought a living through farming while the Métis had been content to develop agriculture only for their immediate use. The Métis prefered to rely on hunting for their livelihood. And the railroad as it was pushed westward also aggravated the economic situation and created what one witness described as an "unhappy boom". So insecure were the Métis in the new ways of life that they became quite unable to cope with them. Their life, which up to then had been taken up by hunting and unlimited liberty, was now restricted to agriculture on a limited acreage. They, who had never known the value of money, whose main staple had been the buffalo hide, were confronted suddenly by the white man's medium of exchange. It is no wonder that many of them sold their lands for a song to avid land speculators. In order to recover his liberty, in order to ensure the stability of the economy he knew, in order to escape the stifling influences of the new civilization, the Métis and his family retreated further into the interior. It seemed to him, as a witness has recorded :

> ... that he could at last find a remedy to his ills and the realization of his hopes in that far place where the horizon merges with the sky.

The Métis settled on the banks of the South Saskatchewan River near Duck Lake and Fort Carlton and in the qu'Appelle valley. They founded such villages as St. Laurent, St. Albert, Sacre-Coeur and St. Antoine de Padoue, the latter becoming famous as "Batoche" during the rebellion. For roughly ten years, the Métis people attempted to obtain from the federal authorities in Ottawa the solution to their political and economic difficulties. Their peaceful agitation was to no avail. The Métis, and for that matter the white settler, needed land. The land was in danger of being taken over by the railway and various other land companies. Not only did they object to a survey which insisted that the lands on which they had settled were part of the land subsidy given to the company now engaged in the building of Canada's first transcontinental; they also objected to the method used in surveying the land. The Métis had been accustomed to a division of land in such a way as to provide a narrow frontage on a river or road for means of transportation. The Métis petitioned for a redress but in vain. In 1882 the land agent at Prince Albert wrote to the Surveyor General of Canada concerning this question :

THE APPRENTICESHIP

> I have the honour to request information as to the possibility of re-surveying these sections into river lots.

Six months after he had written his letter, he received the following answer :

> I have the honour to inform you that it is not the intention of the Government to cause any re-surveys to be made.

The Settlers of St. Albert, who had occupied their lands before the survey had been undertaken, sent a delegation to Ottawa to obtain free land, a registry office, and representation in the legislature. They had some success, at least on a few points, but unfortunately the concessions were not universal and many communities were left without them. The Government was wearied of accepting the Métis' claim that they had the same title to the land as the Indians did because of their Indian mothers. The Government furthermore argued that most of the Métis now complaining in Saskatchewan had already been given free land in Manitoba. Where was it all to stop ? The Government did not feel it its duty to compensate the Métis for having sold their Manitoba land for a song and having had to move. This attitude was unfortunate. The Métis constituted a separate problem in the west — separate from the problem of the white settler and separate from that of the Indian. For one thing, the Métis complained that they were not able to register their claims to their land, and it is a fact that the Métis were not able to register their title to a plot of land before 1881, and at that time only one patent office was opened in Prince Albert. A missionary wrote to Ottawa in 1881 as follows :

> I came to Battleford, urged not only by my own grievances, but by the entreaties of the half-breed population, and they join their earnest prayers to mine to call your special attention to the unsatisfactory state of the lands question in this country. The anxiety of the people of the part of the country where I am is very great, and calls for your immediate consideration.

The petitions continued unabated until finally in the early part of 1884, the Government decided to investigate. They sent Superintendent Pearce. Unfortunately for the majority of the population their claims could not be investigated at that time since they had the misfortune of speaking only French, and as Pearce stated :

> I would have required an interpreter.

Superintendent Pearce therefore sent the land agent of Prince Albert. However the agent was unable to go to Batoche and to St. Laurent until May of 1884 and his report did not reach Ottawa until October of that year. In Ottawa it was apparently buried in the files because no reference is made to it until February of 1885 when the agent was finally instructed to put his recommendations into effect. The concessions of course came too late. The Métis were on the eve of their rebellion. In May of 1884, the discontent was such that a resolution was passed unanimously at a meeting of the French and English-speaking half-breeds of the region. The resolution read as follows :

> ... that a delegation be sent to Louis Riel, and have his assistance to bring all the matters referred to in the above resolutions in a proper shape and form before the Government of Canada, so that our just demands be granted.

But why Riel ? It is true that Riel had led the resistance to Canada's taking over the territories in 1869 and 1870 and had given in only when the Canadian government had granted the specific requests of the Métis. But no one had really heard of him since. He had gone to the province of Quebec, then had moved to Washington, D.C. and he was now a school teacher somewhere in Montana. Archbishop Taché, the Roman Catholic archbishop of Manitoba, explained this summons to Riel as follows :

> This summons was made in the face of the impossibility for the Métis, their friends and others to obtain any form of satisfaction from the federal government. Riel, being one of their own, having suffered with them and for them, would be interested in their cause, which was really his, and success could crown his efforts as it had not so long ago.

The delegation was sent to Montana and the resolution given to Riel. In his reply, Riel stated :

> St. Peter's Mission, Montana, 5th June, 1884.
> To Messrs. James Isbister, Gabriel Dumont, Moise Ouellette, and Michel Dumas.

Gentlemen — You have travelled more than seven hundred miles from the Saskatchewan country, across the international line to make me a visit. The communities in the midst of which you live have sent you as their delegate to ask my advice on various difficulties which have rendered the British North West as yet unhappy under the Ottawa Government. Moreover, you invite me to go and stay amongst you, your hope being that I for one could help to better in some respects your condition. Cordial and pressing is your invitation. You want me and my family to accompany you. I am at liberty to excuse myself and say no. Yet, you are waiting for me, so that I have only to get ready . . .

To be frank is the shortest. I doubt whether my advice given to you on this soil concerning affairs on Canadian territory could cross the borders and retain any influence. But here is another view. The Canadian Government owe me two hundred and fifty acres of land, according to the thirty-first clause of the Manitoba Treaty . . . Those my claims against them are such as to hold good notwithstanding the fact that I have become an American citizen.

Considering, then, your interest and mine, I accept your very kind invitation. I will go and spend some time amongst you. By petitioning the Government with you perhaps we will all have the good fortune of obtaining something. But my intention is to come back early this fall . . .

I have the honour to be, gentlemen delegated to me, your humble servant : Louis Riel.

Riel's arrival in July was hailed as a good omen by all the people of the Territories. At a meeting of the half-breeds at Batoche on July 8th, he spoke as follows :

It is not necessary to be so sad. If we proceed honestly, methodically, and with persistence, it is impossible for the government not to see the justice of our petitions. And then the government will heed them. Patience, calm, and the use of every possible constitutional means : these are the only means to bring to fruition the task we have set out to do.

A few days later, he spoke in the same vein in Prince Albert. Riel's work was to co-ordinate and unite the Métis, the white settlers and the Indians. He founded the Union Métisse de St. Joseph in September of 1884. The Indians he associated with the Métis. And he placated the white settlers by agreeing to their claims that a legislature should be granted for the territories. And so in the summer and early fall of 1884, the agitation was constitutional and legal; at that time there was no intention to wage a rebellion. Through assemblies, petitions, and newspaper editorials the people of the Saskatchewan made their will and needs known to all. However the situation soon deteriorated. There was a crop failure and the government lowered the budget of the Department of the Interior, which was responsible for the Northwest, Moreover, the white settlers and the Roman Catholic clergy began to wonder where all this was going to lead. The white settlers feared that their dominant position would be in jeopardy if they continued their support to Riel, for should Riel win, where would they stand ? And the clergy, fearing a blow to its domination in the Northwest, began to oppose Riel. In July of 1884, a missionary had been able to write to the lieutenant-governor of the territories :

> I am convinced there is not any danger of disturbance. The arrival of Riel has acted as a calm on all the agitated minds, and all his words are to advocate peace and good feelings among all the people in the country.

But in October of 1884, only three months later, the same missionary had reached a much different opinion. He wrote this time :

> Now, Governor, I think it is really the duty of the government to get Riel out of mischief as soon as possible. Riel disappearing, everything will quiet down.

Riel remained and waited. Nothing happened. In February 1885, he suggested that he should return to Montana. A meeting of half-breeds asked him to stay. Riel stayed. The population was exasperated beyond words. Constitutional means having failed, should not a bolder policy be followed ? Riel thought so. On March 19, 1885, when he heard that 500 mounted police were on their way to arrest himself and the other leaders of the agitation, he established a provisional government. The white settlers and the clergy disassociated themselves completely from this illegal move. But Riel was determined that he would continue in his course. The pattern of 1869 repeated itself. Hostage were taken and an ultimatum was sent on March 21 to Major Crozier, the commanding officer of the Canadian force, ordering him to :

> ... give up completely the situation in which the Canadian government have placed you in, at Carlton, and Battleford, together with all government properties.

Crozier replied by demanding the surrender of Riel and his followers. On March 26, 1885, the major gave the order to sound the "boots and saddles" and on this day he and his force marched out of Carlton in order to :

> assert the authority of the Dominion of Canada in the North Saskatchewan.

The rebellion had begun. It was not to last a long time. By May it was all over. However the agitation which followed was worse. Slowly and gradually the Canadian people proceeded on the dangerous path of racial conflict.

# RACIAL CONFLICT 4

## The Aftermath of the 1885 Rebellion

On May 16, 1885, newspapers across Canada announced Louis Riel's surrender. Most of the troops which had been sent out West to put an end to the rebellion returned home. But the trouble had just begun. Although the Canadian people had suppressed the rebellion by a united effort, they were unable to maintain a spirit of national unity. As soon as the immediate danger was past the country became divided on racial lines. The English-language press accused French Canada of disloyalty and of weakening the foundations of Confederation; the French-language press retaliated with an aggressive and militant nationalism. Few attempted to understand or to explain the opinions and convictions of the other side. Quebec was animated by pity and compassion for the Métis leader and for his people. On the other hand, the English-speaking population, as represented by certain factions in Ontario and Quebec, demanded his execution as a traitor. They argued that Riel had already led two rebellions and had endangered Canadian development. Many still remembered the execution in 1870 of the Ontario Orangeman, Thomas Scott, which they felt Riel had not expiated. They were not prepared to let him go unpunished a second time. However, in July 1885 Riel was on trial for leading a rebellion, not for murder. In Quebec there was a crusade to provide an adequate defense for Riel. Three well-known Quebec lawyers were dispatched to defend him.

But many felt that Riel had no chance for they knew that on the jury which would try him there were no Métis, no French Canadians and not even a Roman Catholic.

The trial lasted only an hour and a half, and on August 1, 1885 the jury found Riel guilty of high treason but recommended him to the mercy of the court. Hugh Richardson, the judge, condemned him to be hanged on September 18. The news was received with joy and gratitude in certain sectors of the country, but in Quebec it was met with resentment and consternation. [William Henry Jackson, Riel's private secretary, had been found insane. "Why not Riel?" Quebeckers asked. French Canadians agreed with a newspaper which thundered:

> If insanity is an excuse for an Englishman it must also be one for Riel, even though he is a Métis.

Another paper stated simply:

> Jackson is English; while Riel is a French Canadian. And that's that.]

French Canadians were not to have their way even though they launched a vast campaign to have Riel's sentence commuted to life imprisonment. They argued that Riel was really insane and unable to distinguish between right and wrong.
However, the Canadian government, determined that Riel must hang, was not impressed by the plea of insanity. The government appointed an investigating commission but its terms of reference were such as to prevent any conclusion that would allow the government to recommend mercy. One newspaper asked:

> Has Canada come to the point that in order to maintain its authority, it must raise scaffolds to those unfortunates deprived of their reason ? Must the blood of insane men become the mixture used to cement our national edifice ?

There followed weeks of anxiety, constant petitioning of the government, and soul-searching by French Canadian leaders torn between their duty to their people and their duty to the idea of a united Canada.

The Cabinet was beset with demands for mercy for Riel, while from other parts of the country came the clamour that justice follow its normal course. French-Canadian leaders could easily appreciate the tragic consequences which would follow Riel's execution. Quebec would take a long time to forget. They foresaw that out of this chaos there could be born a movement which could endanger the growth of Confederation. Joseph Israel Tarte, the editor of the prestigious *Le Canadien* wrote :

> At the moment when the corpse of Riel falls through the trap and twists in convulsions of agony, at that moment an abyss will be dug that will separate Quebec from English-speaking Canada, especially Ontario.

The French-Canadian leader most affected was Joseph Adolphe Chapleau, a minister in Sir John A. Macdonald's government, and a young, brilliant and spectacular orator. Considerable pressure was exercised on Chapleau to have him resign his portfolio and lead Quebec in this agitation, and, no doubt, out of Confederation. On the night before he was to sign his assent to the order-in-council ordering Riel's execution, Chapleau summoned to Ottawa three of his trusted lieutenants. One of them related that the four spent all night arguing and weighing the pros and cons of his resignation. Finally at four o'clock in the morning, the three retired, leaving Chapleau to make his momentous decision.

Four hours later they all met at breakfast and, in the words of one of the witnesses :

> Mr. Chapleau, who had not slept, informed us that he had reached the decision not to resign. He gave us his reasons, unperturbed by the emotions of the moment. "We are in the Lions' den", he added. And indeed we were.

Chapleau, describing his decision, wrote to a friend :

> Suddenly I glanced in front of me — in the distance such a sight, tumult, fighting, bloodshed, misery and prostration : and a madman looking from the window of a prison and laughing, rubbing his hands and shouting incoherent words of malediction. I was horrified.

This vision prompted him to assent to Riel's execution. This decision demanded of Chapleau the sacrifice of his personal ambition and a renunciation of his own bitterness towards the government. In a letter to W.W. Lynch, a personal confidant, he stated :

> [I have just thrown the lot in Riel's affair.] In spite of all and many temptations, I have decided to uphold the law and the Crown. I may be sent home for my courage at the next electoral contest. I prefer staying at home to becoming a mob-being... I don't care about having the many with me, if I have the good testimony of my intelligence and conscience. [Tomorrow the storm will rage; I rely upon sunshine at another date. I had thought of yielding to the temptation. There was more than one reason for it. I had so many personal spites to satisfy. I have pocketed all that, and I have done what I thought was my duty.] And if I succumb, I shall retire without grumbling, taking my retreat with dignity. Peace with honour.

In deciding not to resign, Chapleau chose to face the tumult and to fight it. On November 14, came the announcement that Riel was to be hanged. Two days later he was dead. In the Province of Quebec municipal offices flew their flags at half-mast, shopkeepers displayed Riel's picture draped in black in their windows, and the Montreal transport system came to a halt. Men and women carried on their daily tasks in silence, while teachers described to their awe-struck students the vision of a rope dangling in the bitter cold of the prairie. A whole generation vowed hatred to *les maudits Anglais* — "the damned English" — who had perpetrated this judicial murder. On the morning of Riel's execution, the *Mouvement National* was founded by the committees which had been created in many parts of the province to raise funds for Riel's defence and to direct the agitation in favour of clemency.

It was from this organization that the French-Canadian nationalist leader, Honoré Mercier, was later to establish his

Parti National. The *Mouvement* organized protest assemblies all over the province. These were described by the *Toronto Mail* as attempts to institute a French-Canadian dictatorship and to impose what the *Mail* called :

> ... the tyranny of a French minority upon a country consecrated by British blood to British freedom.

In spite of the bombastic pronouncements of the *Mail* and other newspapers, the assemblies continued. On November 22, 1885, the people of Montreal and of the neighbouring district, some led by their parish priests and civic officials, began to assemble in the early hours of the morning on a tract of land known as Le Champ de Mars. Three platforms had been set up around which were grouped about fifty thousand people. French Canada's best orators were present. On that occasion, Wilfrid Laurier, who was to become prime minister eleven years later, declared :

> If I had been on the banks of the Saskatchewan, I too, would have shouldered my musket.

And then looking around him, he asked :

> Where then is Mr. Chapleau ? His place, on this day, is here beside me, on this platform. How many times have I not heard him before he entered politics defending criminals of all sorts ? By the sheer power of his oratory, the jury always found themselves siding with him. Innocent men were saved by him. Gifted, adored by his people, why was he not in Regina defending his compatriot, Louis Riel, that unfortunate man ?

Honoré Mercier stated :

> [Riel our brother is dead, victim of his devotion to the cause of the Métis of whom he was the leader, victim of fanaticism and treason — of the fanaticism of Sir John and some of his friends, of the treason of three of our people who sold their brother to keep their portfolios.] In killing Riel, Sir John Macdonald has not only struck a blow at the heart of our race, but above all he struck the cause of justice and humanity, which, represented in all languages and sanctified by all religious beliefs, begged mercy for the prisoner of Regina, our poor brother of the North-West.

Other speeches followed, and other assemblies. The agitation had become quite dangerous. It was even asserted that Macdonald, the prime minister, was prepared to fight an election

on the issue of Riel if Quebec did not desist from its course
of action. If Macdonald had done so, there is no doubt that
the Province of Quebec would have been isolated from the
rest of the country. It was also true that the English population
would have coalesced against Quebec. The *Toronto Mail*
remarked :

> . . . as the fat crushes the pipkin, so must sheer weight of numbers
> on the English side annihilate the influence of the French minority.

However, the federal parliament had yet to be reckoned with.
In fact, the session of 1886 brought the French-Canadian soul-
searching to a climax. Disappointed and disillusioned, many
Quebec Conservatives were prepared to vote a lack of confidence in the Conservative government. Others had second
thoughts. A vote against the government might still not topple
it. In either case, what would be Quebec's place ? Would it
become the tool of the different parties, forgotten except when
its support was needed ? Many understood this. One of these
was Chapleau. In one of the most remarkable speeches of his
career, he said :

> Mr. Speaker, I regret the execution of the late rebel leader, Louis
> Riel, because I cannot find in my heart a place for a feeling of
> pleasure or rejoicing at the ignominious death of a fellow-being.
> I regret the execution of Louis Riel as I regret those painful
> occasions when a sacrifice of human life has to be made for the
> vindication of the law or for the protection of society. I regret,
> Sir, the execution of Louis Riel because of the unhappy trouble he
> has caused in one of the finest Provinces of this Dominion. [I
> regret the execution of Louis Riel because of the occasion it has
> given for discussion in this House, in which, to use the expression
> of the honorable member for West Durham, "words have been
> said that should not have been said, things have been uttered that
> should not have been uttered, and sentiments have had room for
> expression which should not have been expressed in this House."]
> I regret the execution of Louis Riel for those reasons; but I cannot
> condemn the punishment of his crime.

After having described Riel's actions and having refuted the
comparison of Riel with the *Patriots* of 1837 who took up
arms to defend themselves against the tyranny of the British
majority,* Chapleau concluded :

---

* See the previous volume of this series, "Genesis of a Nation", Chapter 5.

Mr. Speaker, a last word and I address it to those in this House who belong to the same nationality as myself.

Let them beware. [This hour is one of the greatest importance.] Upon them a vast responsibility rests in respect to the vote which they will give to-night upon this question. The future condition of the Province of Quebec will largely depend on the vote which hon. members are about to give. [I have already warned honorable members of the inexpedient attempt which was made to create a so-called political union of all French Canadians throughout the Dominion, and I have said that this was a most unpatriotic step to be taken, that it was one fraught with danger to the Dominion, and fraught with special danger to those who, being a minority in the Dominion, are asked to work together as a unit without considering questions of opinion.

I have often repeated that opinion to my fellow-countrymen. I have often said it, though never so appropriately or so feelingly as I do to-day. In the whole of this agitation I have tried to be true to my country as well as to my duty. I have not followed the dictates of anyone; I have not been biased in my appreciation of facts and things; I have not perhaps followed the path which would be in my own private interest.

No;] the great danger with us is that we shall make a faction of the minority in this country, that we shall make what is called a close political alliance amongst ourselves, but in reality one which would be most unpatriotic and disastrous to the French Canadians.

I ask the honorable members, therefore, [to look at this question as it should be viewed, to look at the laws as they exist, to look at the difficulty of the position in which the Minister of Justice and the Government were placed,] to judge not from feeling nor from the relations of blood or creed or nationality. It is natural with men of one Province or of one blood to feel more warmly in regard to the case of men of their own Province, of their own blood and religion. But we must not judge of this matter in that light. [These have been my sentiments during the last four months. I have not changed my mind to suit men and circumstances; I have relied upon the reward given to men who do not flinch before the cries of the multitude, and who do not seek their political fortune in the success of the moment. I have walked straight before me in what I thought was the right path as a citizen of Canada. I have followed that conduct, I have not been biased, and in the whole of what I have done, in the whole of what I have said through that painful crisis, I trust I have not lost the sympathies of my friends, the respect of my enemies, nor the confidence of the country.]

Across the aisle from Chapleau, was Wilfrid Laurier, the Liberal French-Canadian leader. On the occasion of this debate, Laurier made one of his greatest speeches. He began by stating:

Sir, I am not of those who look upon Louis Riel as a hero. Nature had endowed him with many brilliant qualities, but nature denied him that supreme quality without which all other qualities, however brilliant, are of no avail. Nature denied him a well-balanced mind. [At his worst he was a subject fit for an asylum; at his best he was a religious and political monomaniac.] But he was not a bad man — I do not believe at least that he was the bad man he has been represented to be in a certain press. But that he was insane appears to me beyond the possibility of controversy. When the reports first came here last spring and in the early summer of his doings and sayings in the North-West, when we heard that he was to depose the Pope and establish an American Pope, those who did not know him believed he was an imposter, but those who knew him knew at once what was the matter. In the Province of Quebec there was not an instant's hesitation about it. Almost every man in that province knew that he had been several times confined in asylums, and therefore it was manifest to the people of Quebec that he had fallen into one of those misfortunes with which he was afflicted. When his counsel were engaged and commenced to prepare his trial, they saw at once that if justice to him and only justice was to be done, their plea should be a plea of insanity.

Then after having questioned the fairness of the trial, Laurier concluded :

But to-day, [not to speak of those who have lost their lives,] our prisons are full of men who, despairing ever to get justice by peace, sought to obtain it by war, who, despairing of ever being treated like freemen, took their lives in their hands, rather than be treated as slaves. They have suffered a great deal, they are suffering still; yet their sacrifices will not be without reward. Their leader is in the grave, they are in durance, but from their prisons they can see that that justice, that liberty which they sought in vain, and for which they fought in vain, has at last dawned upon their country.

[Their fate well illustrates the truth of Byron's invocation to liberty, in the introduction to the Prisoner of Chillon :

Eternal Spirit of the chainless mind !
Brightest in dungeons, Liberty thou art !
For these they habitation is the heart —
The heart which love of thee alone can bind;
And when they sons to fetters are consigned —
To fetters and the damp vault's dayless gloom,
Their country conquers with their martyrdom.

Yes, their country has conquered with their martyrdom. They are in durance to-day; but the rights for which they were fighting have been acknowledged. We have not the report of the commission yet, but we know that more than two thousand claims so long denied have been at last granted. And more — still more.]

> We have it in the Speech from the Throne that at last representation
> is to be granted to those Territories. This side of the House long
> sought, but sought in vain, to obtain that measure of justice. It
> could not come then, but it came after the war; it came as the
> last conquest of that insurrection. [And again I say that their
> country has conquered with their martyrdom,] and if we look at
> that one fact alone there was cause sufficient, independent of all
> others, to extend mercy to the one who is dead and to those
> who live.

At the conclusion of the debate, on March 24, 1886, 16 Conservatives from the Province of Quebec voted against the Government — against their own party — while 23 chose to remain within the ranks of the party. The matter was officially over.

Yet the Riel affair had grave implications for the future. The fraternal identification with Riel and the fears of French Canada would be forgotten with the passage of time, but political leaders would not forget the limit of their power which the affair had revealed. The French-Canadian ministers had not been able to influence their colleagues. The representatives of Quebec had not succeeded in compelling the government to answer the almost unanimous demands of their people. To restore the political influence of their province, they had to make humiliating compromises. In the years to come many were to remember the lessons of 1885. Parliament in Ottawa was finished with the matter, but the agitation continued unabated at the provincial level.

A little more than a year after the federal government had disposed of the matter an election was held in the province of Quebec. The campaign was based largely on the Riel affair, and the so-called treason of those who accepted Ottawa's decision. In January, 1887, Honoré Mercier's Liberals won the election, defeating the Conservative government. Mercier was to remain Premier of Quebec for the next 15 years — until 1892, when he would be dismissed by the lieutenant-governor for corruption.

Mercier was in more ways than one a giant. He was a fiery French-Canadian nationalist dedicated to the task of building a strong province of Quebec. That need was great. Rebuffed at

Ottawa, more and more French Canadians were turning to Quebec for the protection they needed. Mercier became the embodiment of their task. Yet in many ways, he was a demagogue; for he was a man determined to build a political party on prejudice, hatred and wrath. This was certainly his method in the famous controversy over the Jesuit Estates Bill. During the French régime in Canada the Jesuit order had received vast tracts of land in Quebec. When New France was conquered, Great Britain confiscated these properties. With Confederation, in 1867, they became the properties of the province of Quebec, which used the revenue from the lands, about $20,000 a year, for educational purposes. But the Quebec ecclesiastical authorities had been agitating for their return to Church control. And within the church itself, the Jesuit order, the original owners of the lands, had been claiming the right to their ownership. Under Mercier's "Jesuit Estates Bill" the religious authorities were to receive $400,000 for the lands. No one less than the Pope was to decide how the money would be divided among the Jesuit order and the province's ecclesiastical authorities.

The bill had national repercussions. It aroused a violent reaction from the Protestants — supported by the Equal Rights Association, the Orange Lodge and many Ontario newspapers. One of these papers reported that a clergyman in Ontario had been heard to suggest that :

... the assassination of the Jesuits would be welcomed by heaven.

What many objected to was the preamble to the Act, which gave the Pope the power to divide the $400,000. A campaign was launched to force the federal government to disallow the provincial legislation on the grounds that a foreign power had supplanted the authority of the British Crown and that the public treasury was being depleted to compensate individuals who had no legal right to restitution. It was further argued that the Act infringed upon the separation of Church and State and that the secularization of the Church lands which had taken place some 40 years previously had settled the question of clerical estates for once and for all. Anti-Catholic sentiment was probably at the root of all these protests. If proof of this is needed, consider the following, an excerpt from a pamphlet written by a Protestant clergyman from Ontario:

[This Papal Hierarchy, called a "church", however, we find is not only tolerated in Canada, it is patronized ! A few years ago the Government of this country, which has recently endowed Romanism and the Jesuits, refused to incorporate the Orangemen as a body of Protestants in a Protestant Country ! and now, forsooth, in this same Protestant Country, they consent to the incorporation and endowment of the Jesuits as a steadily increasing and presistently encroaching anti-Protestant body of Roman Catholics ! One would think that they were, upon each occasion, in session at a particular phase of the moon, and were, in consequence, laboring under at least temporary insanity ! Denying this, however, it certainly lays them, one and all, open to a very serious impeachment of their motives.] Romanism has no rights in Canada, or upon any British, or Protestant territory. It has by its iniquitous, cruel, and bloody deeds against Protestants of the past; by its unannulled canons and published atrocious principles and aims of the present; by the well-known Syllabus of Pope Pius 9, which embodies all those atrocious principles; by the still more recent Jesuitical Encyclicals of Pope Leo 13; and by its ceaseless, undying, inextinguishable aim at universal sovereignty, temporal and spiritual, and the extirpation of all opposing supremacies, civil as well as religious, it has, I say, by such papistically approved principles, aims, and doings forfeited all claim to be recognized as having any rights whatever in any Protestant country.

In the Federal parliament Prime Minister Macdonald explained his decision not to disallow the provincial legislation :

I hope and believe that when this matter is fully understood in the Province of Ontario, when the exhaustive speeches that were made upon it are read and discussed and weighed, the country will see that their apprehensions are unfounded, and that the country is safe. Why, there are in all the Dominion of Canada 71 Jesuits. Are they going to conquer the whole of Canada ? Is Protestantism to be subdued ? Is the Dominion to be seduced from its faith by 71 Jesuit priests ? They are armed with a string of beads, a sash around their waists and a mass book or missal. What harm can they do ? I told my reverend and eloquent friend, Dr. Potts of Toronto, that I would match him physically and spiritually, against any follower of Ignatius Loyola in the whole Dominion of Canada. Now, only think of it. The Jesuits claimed, and claimed with an appearance of right, that the effect of their restoration should be to give them back all their own property. They contended for that, and they had the right to fight the best battle they could. Look at the papers. They said that the value of the property was $2,000,000, but they came down, however, graciously, and said they would take $1,000,000, or, to be accurate, I think,

$900,000. But the Government of the Province of Quebec said : No, you cannot have that; you can only have $400,000 — not a very large sum. [Why Mr. Mercier has been granting, in the interest of his country, sums as big as that for railways here and there through Quebec. We do the same thing here.] It is no very large sum. But not only did Mr. Mercier confine the vote to $400,000 but he said : You shall have not the whole of it; perhaps you shall have none of it.

The other ecclesiastic institutions, Catholic colleges, said they had a right to their share. Now, it was a family matter, it was *in foro domestico,* and as the honorable member for Bothwell (Mr. Mills) truly said, it was their own money, it was the property of the Province of Quebec and they could do with it as they liked . . . Believing as we do that it is perfectly within the competence of that Legislature, and does not in any way affect any other portion of Her Majesty's dominions, there would be no excuse for our interfering . . .

Supposing this Bill had been disallowed, Mr. Mercier would have gained a great object. He would have been the champion of his Church. The moment it was announced that this Bill was disallowed there would have been a summons for a meeting of the Legislature of Quebec. They would have passed that Bill unanimously, and would have sent it back here, and what would have been the consequence ? Agitation, a quarrel — a racial and a religious war would be aroused. The best interests of the country would be prejudiced, our credit would be ruined abroad, and our social relations destroyed at home. I cannot sufficiently picture, in my faint language, the misery and the wretchedness which would have been heaped upon Canada if this question, having been agitated as it has been, and would be, had culminated in a series of disallowances of this Act.

And there the matter rested. At least constitutionally. But not politically. The Riel crisis had served to awaken French Canadian nationalism and to coalesce its forces. The Jesuit Estates controversy served to test its aggressiveness. Just as French Canadians were not to forget the lessons of the Riel affair, many English-speaking Canadians were not to forget those of the Jesuit Estates.

It was as a direct result of the Francophobia, anti-clericalism, and anti-Catholicism which has been raised by the agitation over the Jesuits Estates that a campaign was launched in Western Canada, especially in Manitoba, to deprive the French Canadians and Catholics of their constitutional rights to language and to the maintenance of their schools. The die was cast. Canada was never to be the same.

# CHURCH AND STATE      *5*

## *Quebec Politics in the Decade Following Confederation*

One of the effects of Confederation — the union of the British North American colonies into the Dominion of Canada — was to increase the tension which had always existed between the Church and the government in the Province of Quebec. Under the federal system created by Confederation in 1867, Quebec, like the other provinces, received wide powers to look after its own affairs — those which did not affect the new Dominion as a whole.

Certain people in Quebec argued that under Confederation the Church's power had been increased. Their argument went something like this : Since the majority in Quebec are Roman Catholic, and since under Confederation the province of Quebec had a considerable degree of autonomy, Confederation had therefore indirectly recognized the favoured position of the Roman Catholic Church in Quebec. What is more, they argued, Confederation imposed upon all French-Canadian politicians not only the responsibility of framing any new legislation in accordance with the canons of the Church, but also the duty of amending existing laws when called upon to do so by the Church.

Quebeckers who thought along these lines believed that under Confederation Quebec formed a state within a state, that it had an established church, and that political decisions were subject to ecclesiastical directives and scrutiny. To remind people that the ecclesiastical authorities had a considerable voice in political matters, and to assist them in the exercise of their rights as electors the Bishop of Montreal once advised his flock :

> Let each say in his heart, I hear my curé, my curé hears the bishop, the bishop hears the Pope, and the Pope hears our Lord Jesus Christ.

Many French Canadians were opposed to this degree of clerical intervention. They believed that an extreme clericalism in politics would provoke a Protestant reaction and serve as a pretext for discriminating against French Canadians in other provinces, where they were in a minority. In fact, Alexander Tilloch Galt, the traditional leader of the Quebec Protestants, did fear for his people and had suggested that :

> A deep laid plan exists for the complete subjugation of Quebec to ecclesiastical rule, with the view of extending the same baneful existence, hereafter, to the whole "Dominion".

However, T. White, a journalist and a Conservative and Protestant politician denied Galt's fears. He wrote :

> The position of the Protestant minority in Quebec is one surrounded by some difficulty; but, as yet, there is nothing to indicate that it is one of danger. Our true interest, I venture to think, is to keep a strict watchfulness over our own rights, to be ever ready to maintain them, if they should be attacked, and to preserve towards the religious majority a position of absolute neutrality, in so far as the religious disputes of that majority are concerned.
>
> With an abstinence from interference in those disputes, and continuing our alliances on political grounds alone, the Protestants of the Province will best maintain our own rights, and most certainly minister to the best interest of the state.

Yet, the fear was genuine, and it was even shared by many Roman Catholics, who made a distinction between the clergy's role as a teaching body and the clergy as ordinary citizens. Clerical authority, this group said, could only be exercised in matters involving moral and religious principles. Priests were entitled to attempt to influence the political opinions of the people, and because of their respected position in French Canadian society this influence was considerable. But they had no *authority* in this field; they did not have to be obeyed. There was nothing new about this distinction, and it was even in accordance with episcopal teachings. But it was often ignored, especially in the 1870's when the episcopacy and the clergy came to the conclusion that the Liberal Party constituted a moral evil which had to be eradicated from French-Canadian society.

The Liberal party, which had made considerable gains in elections of 1874 and 1875, was said to be influenced by European radical movements. It was the heir of the pre-Confederation Liberal Party which had talked about liberty of conscience and of the press, and had advocated the abolition of tithes. The ecclesiastical authorities never felt very much at home in a room where there were many Liberals.

The Liberals, to further their cause, founded newspapers and clubs. One of the most important of the clubs was the Institut Canadien, founded as early as 1848 — nineteen years before Confederation. By 1867, the year of Confederation, every prominent Liberal in Montreal belonged to the Institut Canadien, which was engaged in a dispute with Bishop Bourget on the question of forbidden books in their library.

After the dispute had continued for two years, the Bishop appealed to Rome, and then issued a directive condemning the *Institut* and ordering all Catholics to give up their membership — or else face excommunication.

Shortly afterwards the Liberals were given the opportunity to prove that they refused to be intimidated in this manner. A member of the *Institut,* Joseph Gibord, died without making his peace with the Church. The authorities refused to bury him in the consecrated ground where he had already bought a plot. His widow, influenced by the Liberals, brought the matter before the courts. For five years the courts debated, and after a series of appeals the case ended up with the judicial committee of the Privy Council of England, the highest tribunal in the empire. The Privy Council ruled in favour of the widow. At first the church authorities refused to comply, but a court order forced them to do so.

The incident demonstrated that the Liberals were determined to challenge clerical immunity, ecclesiastical prerogatives, and above all, the idea that the Church was independent of state control.

The Church was determined to fight, and it found its partner in the Conservative Party, or rather an extreme wing of the Conservative Party. This group, in 1871, had issued a manifesto known as the "Catholic Program". This remarkable document begins with the declaration of allegiance in principle to the Conservative Party as :

> The only defender of social authority and the only one offering serious guaranties to religious interests.

Under the Catholic Program, Conservatives were required to harmonize provincial and federal legislation with the doctrines of the Roman Catholic church.

Therefore the program laid down four rules to assist the electors in the exercise of their franchise :

> 1. If the contest is between two Conservatives, it goes without saying that we shall support the one who accepts the program we have just outlined.
>
> 2. If on the contrary it is between a Conservative of any shade whatever and an adept of the Liberal school, our active sympathies will be given to the former.
>
> 3. If the only candidates who come forward in a constituency are both Liberals or oppositionists, we must choose the one who will accept our conditions.
>
> 4. Finally, in the event that the contest is between a Conservative who rejects our program and an opportunist who accepts it, the position would be more delicate. To vote for the latter would be

to imperil the Conservative Party, which we wish to see powerful. What decision should we make between these two dangers ? In this case we would advise Catholic electors to refrain from voting.

The aim of the program was to create a group of politicians willing to put aside party discipline when the issue involved a religious matter. Even though this program was widely criticized and not *wholly* accepted either by the Church or the Conservative Party, by 1875 it became the fundamental platform of the Conservative Party for Quebec and remained so for a time. It seemed that everyone had come to agree with an Alsatian Jesuit who once stated during a religious ceremony in Montreal :

> The Church can request the government to grant civil sanction to its laws, but this sanction adds nothing to the right of the law, but merely facilitates it.

> The Church does not submit bills, projected laws, to the government; but a law which is already an obligation of conscience.
> It is not for the government to revise these laws, to discuss them, or to change them; it has not jurisdiction.

> The Church alone possesses the right to judge ecclesiastical cases, to dispose of matrimonial cases, and to prescribe the formalities therefor. The Church enjoys these immunities, and whoever dares to interfere is guilty of sacrilege.

> Governments often aid in the establishment of parishes, but as a favour and not as a right, and they enjoy this right only when it is given them by the Holy Father. If the government should presume to aid in the establishment of parishes without the permission of the Holy See, it would be guilty of an act of sacrilege.

> Such are the truths which your pastor has caused to triumph. They assure the submission of the State to the Church, and the State dependent upon the Church will be submissive to God. At the moment we may see throughout Europe Catholics vying with one another, with the encouragement of the Holy See, to fight those who seek to hamper the liberty of the Church, and to elect to office those right-thinking men who promise to defend the rights of the Church.

> Similarly on many occasions the Bishop of Montreal has exhorted the faithful to vote for men who are determined to fight error and to protect the Church and its rights.

> And may you, brethren, be always one with your bishop in the battles against error. As a general guides his army, your pastor leads you... Remember that he has caused to triumph the infallibility and independence of the Church, the subordination of the State to the Church.

That the bishops had come to consider the Liberals a fundamental threat to the authority of the Church is demonstrated in a pastoral letter published in September 1875, which read in part as follows :

> Distrust above all that liberalism which wishes to cover itself with the fine name of "Catholic" in order to accomplish more easily its criminal mission. You will recognize it easily from the description which the Sovereign Pontiff has often given of it :
>
> (1)  The endeavour to subordinate the Church to the State;
>
> (2)  Incessant attempts to break the bonds which unite the children of the Church with one another and with their clergy;
>
> (3)  The monstrous alliance of truth with error under the pretext of reconciling all things and avoiding conflicts;
>
> (4)  Finally, the illusion, or at times the hypocrisy, which conceals a boundless pride under the mask of religion and of a fine assurance of submission to the Church ... No one, therefore, may in the future with good conscience be permitted to remain a Catholic liberal.

In that pastoral letter the bishops did not name the Liberal Party. When they condemned "liberalism" they were using the term in a general sense. When they referred to "Catholic liberals" they spelled "liberal" with a small "l".

Nevertheless, their episcopal letter was interpreted by the majority of the clergy and by the Conservative press as an attack against the Liberal Party and a condemnation of all who belonged to it. As soon as a candidate declared himself to be in favour of the Liberal government in Ottawa or opposed to the Conservative government in Quebec he became a "Catholic Liberal" who should be condemned by the religious authorities.

The Liberals felt that the clergy's interference in politics to this extent deprived the electors of their freedom of choice.

Once more the Liberals went to court to prove their position. This time the case involved the election of a Conservative politician, Hector Langevin, in a federal by-election in the constituency of Charlevoix.

During the election campaign priest after priest had denounced liberalism. They invoked the horrors of the French Revolution and explained to their awe-struck parishioners that the contest in Charlevoix was really a contest between the Pope on the one side, and the forces of anticlericals who killed priests and raped nuns, on the other.

The Liberals protested to the courts, and thirteen months after the election the Supreme Court of Canada ruled that Langevin had not, in effect, been "elected", for the Catholic electors of Charlevoix could not be considered to have been free in the exercise of their franchise since they had been subjected to intimidation. In other words, a civil authority had ruled that clerical interference in politics rendered the democratic form of government inoperative.

Fortunately, this ruling came at about the same time as an important action within the church itself. After much pressure from Quebec politicians and even members of the clergy, Rome decided to send an apostolic delegate to investigate the entire problem. He arrived, in the person of Bishop Conroy, the bishop of Ardagh, Ireland, on May 24, 1877.

The bishop had hardly had time to begin his investigation before Wilfrid Laurier, leader of the French-Canadian Liberals, delivered his now famous speech on political liberalism. This speech climaxed the trend towards moderation within the Liberal Party — a trend which had been increasing in the ten years since Confederation.

The purpose of Laurier's address was to define the ideas and principles of Canadian liberalism. He hoped to be able to remove the prejudices and the opposition of those who believed that liberalism was heresy in faith and revolution in politics.

> I know that in the eyes of a large number of my fellow countrymen, the Liberal party is a party composed of men of perverse doctrines and dangerous tendencies, pressing knowingly and deliberately towards revolution. I know that in the eyes of a portion of my fellow countrymen the Liberal party is a party of men of upright intentions, perhaps, but victims and dupes of principles which are leading them unconsciously but fatally towards revolution. In short, I know that in the eyes of another and not the least considerable portion, perhaps, of our people, Liberalism is a new form of evil, a heresy carrying with it its own condemnation.

Yet political liberalism was not Catholic liberalism for as Laurier stated :

In our adversaries' party it is the custom to accuse us Liberals of irreligion. I am not here to parade my religious sentiments, but I declare that I have too much respect for the faith in which I was born ever to use it as the basis of a political organization. You wish to organize a Catholic party ... to organize all the Catholics into one party, without other bond, without other basis, than a common religion. Have you not reflected that by that very fact you will organize the Protestant population as a single party, and then, instead of the peace and harmony now prevailing between the different elements of the Canadian people, you throw open the door to war, a war of religion, the most terrible of all wars ? Our adversaries further reproach us ... with denying to the Church, the freedom to which it is entitled. They reproach us with seeking to silence the administrative body of the Church, and to prevent it from teaching the people their duties as citizens and electors. They reproach us with wanting to hinder the clergy from sharing in politics and to relegate them to the sacristy. In the name of the Liberal party and of Liberal principles, I repel this assertion. I maintain that there is not one Canadian Liberal who wants to prevent the clergy from taking part in political affairs if they wish to do so.

In the name of what principle should the friends of liberty seek to deny to the priest the right to take part in political affairs ? In the name of what principle should the friends of liberty seek to deny to the priest the right to have and to express political opinions, the right to approve or disapprove public men and their acts, and to instruct the people in what he believes to be their duty ? In the name of what principle should he not have the right to say that if I am elected religion will be endangered, when I have the right to say that if my adversary is elected, the state will be endangered ? ... No. Let the priest speak and preach as he thinks best; such is his right and no Canadian Liberal will dispute that right ... [Everyone has the right not only to express his opinion, but to influence, if he can, by the expression of his opinion, the opinion of his fellow-citizens. This right exists for all, and there can be no reason why the priest should be deprived of it. I am here to speak my whole mind, and I may add that I am far from finding opportune the intervention of the clergy in the domain of politics, as it has been exercised for some years.] I believe, [on the contrary,] that from the standpoint of the respect due his character, the priest has everything to lose by meddling in the ordinary questions of politics; still, his right to do so is indisputable, and if he thinks proper to use it, our duty, as Liberals, is to guarantee it to him against all denial.

This right, however, is not unlimited. We have no absolute right among us. The rights of each man, in our state of society, end precisely where they encroach upon the rights of others.

The right of interference in politics ends where it would encroach upon the elector's independence . . .

The constitution of the country rests on the freely expressed will of every elector . . . It is perfectly legitimate to alter the elector's opinion by argument and all other means of persuasion, but never by intimidation. As a matter of fact, persuasion changes the elector's conviction; intimidation does not . . . If the opinion expressed by the majority of the electors is not their real opinion, but an opinion snatched from them by fraud, by threats or by corruption, the constitution is violated; you have not government by the majority but government by the minority.

I am not one of those who parade themselves as friends and champions of the clergy. However, I say this : like most of my young fellow-countrymen, I have been educated by priests and among young men who have become priests. I flatter myself that I have among them some sincere friends, and to them at least I can and do say : Consider whether there is under the sun a country happier than our own; consider whether there is under the sun a country where the Catholic Church is free or more privileged than it is here. [Why then should you, by claiming rights incompatible with our state of society, expose this country to agitations of which the consequences are impossible to foresee ?

But I address myself also to all my fellow-countrymen without distinction, and to them I say :] We are a free and happy people, and we are so owing to the liberal institutions by which we are governed, institutions which we owe to the exertions of our fore-fathers and the wisdom of the mother country. The policy of the Liberal party is to protect these institutions, to defend and extend them, and, under their sway, to develop the latent resources of our country. That is the policy of the Liberal party : it has no other.

For the next few months after Wilfrid Laurier delivered that speech, the apostolic delegate, Bishop Conroy, continued his investigation into the strained relations between Liberals and clergy in Quebec. The official instructions he had received from the Holy See ordered him :

> . . . (To establish) a uniform line of conduct, that each and all should adhere to in their relations with political parties.

The Vatican authorities wanted Bishop Conroy to make it clear to the Canadian clergy that the papal condemnation of Catholic liberalism did not include a censure of all political parties which happened to have the name "Liberal", but was directed only at parties which were opposed to Christian doctrines.

His instructions included the comment that :

> All those acted wrongly who, without other result, declared that the Church condemned one of the political parties in Canada... a party which has already been warmly supported by some of the bishops themselves.

Bishop Conroy was warned, when studying the questions of clerical influence on electors, and the bringing of priests before civil courts, to :

> ...act with caution. There would be no need to question the competence of the civil courts if priests would never mention either party by name and never use the influence of their ministry to condemn a party or politician, except when either was inimical to the true interest of the Church.

Bishop Conroy spent five months visiting eastern and central Canada. He talked with bishops, priests, nuns, politicians, judges, and ordinary citizens. He instructed priests of the constituency of Gaspé, through their bishop, not to interfere in a by-election there, and to admit Liberals to the sacraments. When he visited the Liberal prime minister, Alexander Mackenzie, in June, he shocked him by telling him that the Liberal party had been represented to Rome as :

> "...an extreme revolutionary party closely related to the Red Republican communes of France and Italy."

Every day a mass of documents — proposals, counterproposals, accusations and justifications, appeared on Bishop Conroy's desk. Liberals, Conservatives, and members of the clergy had been insisting all through the summer of 1877 that a division among the bishops made imperative an early official decision as to which of the bishops were right and which wrong. In September, convinced that, in his own words,

> Some statement from an authority is absolutely necessary...

Bishop Conroy summoned all the Quebec bishops to a meeting in Montreal. A few days later, on October 11, 1877, their excellencies issued a political directive. The new episcopal letter referred to previous ones on the subject of politics. The bishops claimed that they had been misunderstood. They said that, far from abandoning the region of principles to descend into the arena of politics, they were followers of :

> The example of the Holy See, which, in condemning the errors of Catholic liberalism, has always refrained from mentioning persons or political parties. There exist in effect no pontifical acts which condemn whatever political parties. Following the example of the Holy Father, we leave to the conscience of each to judge under the eye of God, and to determine which men are condemned by the pontifical statements, whatever their political party may be.

This episcopal letter did not put an end to the struggle between the Church and the politicians in Quebec; it created an interlude during which the clergy did not interfere, officially, in political matters. This interlude lasted for almost two decades — until the federal election of 1896, in which the question of public funds for Catholic schools became the main issue. Then the struggle was to burst forth once more, and more violently than ever. When the smoke and dust of that battle had settled, Canada had entered a new era.

But that is the subject of another program.

# "THE ARCHITECT"

6

## The Life and Work of
## Sir John A. Macdonald

It has become a cliché of Canadian history to describe Sir John A. Macdonald, the first prime minister, as the "architect" of Canada.

Nevertheless the term is an apt one. It was Macdonald's political insight which brought about the confederation of the British North American colonies in the first place, and it was his ability to compromise, his genuine love for his country and his countrymen, and his deep awareness of his mission which maintained Canada from Confederation, in 1867, until his death a quarter century later.

It was on the foundation which Macdonald established that subsequent prime ministers built their Canada.

The cornerstone of the foundation which Macdonald laid was what he called his "National Policy". This was a three-pronged attack on Canada's economic problems. It consisted of, first :

a policy of protection to Canadian industries through high tariffs on American and other foreign products; second : the building of a transcontinental railway; and third : the development of the vast Canadian west.

On the first of these Macdonald spoke forcefully and at length in a remarkable speech to the House of Commons on March 7, 1878. At the time Macdonald was leader of the opposition; six months later he would be re-elected prime minister. Here is how he described the Canadian economic predicament which led to his belief in the need for protective tariffs :

> We have no manufactures here. We have no work-people; our work-people have gone off to the United States. They are to be found employed in the Western States, in Pittsburgh, and, in fact, in every place where manufactures are going on.
>
> These Canadian artizans are adding to the strength, to the power, and to the wealth, of a foreign nation instead of adding to ours. Our work-people in this country, on the other hand, are suffering for want of employment. Have not their cries risen to Heaven ? Has not the honorable the Premier been surrounded and besieged, even in his own Department, and on his way to his daily duties, by suffering artizans who keep crying out : "We are not beggars, we only want an opportunity of helping to support ourselves and our families." [ Is not such the case also in Montreal and in Quebec ? In fact, is not that the state of things which exists in every part of Canada as well as in the United States ? But this must also be borne in mind, that, when the depression is over and times become prosperous, there will be found manufactures in the United States where men will be required to work. The manufactories and the men are there, but we have not got them here.] If we had a protective system in this country, if we had a developed capital, we could, by giving our manufacturers a reasonable hold on our home trade, attain a higher position among the nations. If our factories were fenced round to a certain extent with protection, and we imposed a tariff ... such as the necessities of Canada may demand, our national prosperity would be enhanced ... If our manufacturers had a reasonable Protection, if they had a hold upon our four million people in the same way as the manufacturers in the United States, then there would be a basis whereby they might be enabled to go in by degrees and develop their resources like those of the United States.
>
> So long as we have a Free-trade system, we can only have substantially one description of industry, and that is — agriculture. Agriculture must be, and will be in our time, at all events, and for many ages, the back-bone of the Dominion of Canada. It will be a chief, a paramount interest. [That interest claims and requires in this country as in the United States, a home market. No

country has ever risen to any rank in the scale of nations or civilization which possessed but one industry. That may, perhaps, be a proposition too broad with respect to manufactures, because we know that nations have risen to rank which had but few manufactures. But if, from the limit of their territorial extent they had no agricultural population, they were soon swept away. Carthage fell because it was only a manufacturing and commercial country. Athens fell for the same reason. So also with Genoa and the Hantz towns. All these merely manufacturing States, which were confined, from the smallness of their extent, to trade and commerce, were swept away because larger and more powerful nations overcame them.] But no nation has arisen which had only agriculture as its industry. There must be a mixture of industries to bring out the national mind and the national strength and to from a national character . . .

Every man is not fitted to be a farmer, to till the soil; one man has a constructive genius, another is an artist, another has an aptitude for trade, another is a skilful mechanic — all these men are to be found in a nation, and, if Canada has only one branch of industry to offer them, if these men cannot find an opportunity in their own country to develop the skill and genius with which God has gifted them, they will go to a country where their abilities can be employed, as they have gone from Canada to the United States.

Six months after he made that speech, Macdonald's Conservative party again became the government — after the elections of 1878.

Parliament opened on February 13, 1879. In the budget speech of 1879 a new tariff, which was fairly high, was established. Canada had launched herself into a nationalistic commercial program.

The second prong of Macdonald's "National Policy" was the building of the trans-continental railway. We saw in an earlier program how Macdonald's fortitude, his determination, and his awareness of political realities made it possible for him to conclude satisfactorily this gigantic undertaking on behalf of the Canadian people. In the midst of the financial difficulties of the Canadian Pacific Railway he had written to the Governor-General in January, 1884 :

"We are going to stand by the CPR, but anticipate great opposition in Parliament, and fear some defection of old friends, but we shall face the opposition manfully."

Facing the opposition manfully was of course a thing which Macdonald had done for many years. By doing so in the matter of the Canadian Pacific he managed to overcome all opposition, and can be considered the builder of the Canadian Pacific Railway.

The third prong of Macdonald's "National Policy" was the development of the West. The dream had been to be able to settle the West as quickly as possible. Its agricultural produce would be brought by a Canadian railway to the East for shipment to Europe and elsewhere, and in turn a Canadian railway would bring back to the West the industrial products of the East. The three-pronged National Policy was in effect an economic unity. If one part of it failed the other two would not be very successful. Unfortunately the settlement of the West did not proceed as quickly as had been anticipated. By the time of Macdonald's death only 250,000 people lived in the territory which is now occupied by the provinces of Manitoba, Saskatchewan and Alberta.

Failure to settle the West means that the railway was not really a profitable venture during the days of Macdonald. Nor did the protection to Canadian industry increase to any great extent the volume of Canada's industrial output. However, it must be remembered that most of the time Macdonald was in office the entire world was in a state of economic depression. Macdonald's political opponents, of course, blamed the bad times on his policies. Here, for example, is how Edward Blake, one of the leaders of the Liberal party, criticized Macdonald's "National Policy" in a speech to the West Durham Reform Convention on March 5, 1891 :

> Its real tendency has been, as foretold twelve years ago, towards disintegration and annexation, instead of consolidation and the maintenance of that British connection of which they claim to be the special guardians. It has left us with a small population, a scanty immigration, and a North-West empty still; with enormous additions to our public debt [and yearly charge], an extravagant system of expenditure, and an unjust and oppressive tariff; with restricted markets for our needs, whether to buy or sell, and all those evils [(greatly intensified by our special conditions)] thence arising; with trade diverted from its natural into forced, and there-

fore, less profitable channels, and with unfriendly relations and frowning tariff walls, ever more and more estranging us from the mighty English-speaking nation to the south — our neighbours and relations — with whom we ought to be, as it was promised that we should be, living in generous amity and liberal intercourse. Worse; far worse ! It has left us with lowered standards of public virtue and a death-like apathy in public opinion; with racial, religious, and provincial animosities rather inflamed than soothed; with a subservient Parliament, an autocratic Executive, debauched constituencies, and corrupted and corrupting classes; with lessened self-reliance and increased dependence on the public chest and on legislative aids, and possessed withal by a boastful jingo spirit far enough removed from true manliness, loudly proclaiming unreal conditions and exaggerated sentiments, while actual facts and genuine opinions are suppressed. It has left us with our hands tied, our future compromised, and in such a plight that, whether we stand or move, we must run some risks which else we might have either declined or encountered with greater promise of success . . .

The record of Macdonald's years is not as bleak as his opponents tried to make it appear. His tariff policy did stimulate Canada's infant industries to the point where they were able to compete in an area largely dominated by the United States. The Canadian Pacific Railway *was* built, and although it did not lead to the immediate population boom in the West which Macdonald had hoped for, it prepared the way for the success of the Liberal government in this field after 1896.

During all these years Macdonald was also confronted by the problems resulting from the racial, cultural and religious diversity of Canada. We have seen in previous programs how the Riel Rebellion in the west and the Jesuit Estates Act in Quebec increased the tension in English-French relations in the new nation.

Macdonald is often criticized for his policy towards the French Canadians, and especially for his handling of the Riel controversy. But anyone who has studied his career realizes that Macdonald always believed that the cultural duality of Canada had to be accepted as a prime condition of its continued existence. He once said :

There is no paramount race in this country, there is no conquered race in this country; we are all British subjects, and those who are not English are none the less British subjects on that account.

He felt that the whole racial cry should be forgotten. He told the House in 1890 :

> Let us forget this cry and we shall have our reward in seeing this unfortunate fire which has been kindled from so small a spark, extinguished forever, and we shall go on, as we have been going on since 1867, as one people, with one object, looking to one future, and expecting to lay the foundation of one great country.

Another source of immense difficulty for Macdonald during these years was what has been called "the revolt of the provinces."

Canada is a federation of provinces which possess certain powers and which must obtain revenue to exercise these powers. The provinces, in the midst of their own economic difficulties, looked upon Ottawa as an immense centralizer which was determined to break them.

Manitoba was angry because it was not allowed to build railways south of the Canadian Pacific line. Nova Scotia, furious because it considered the subsidies granted to it to be inadequate, threatened to secede from the Dominion. Quebec and Ontario were both at open war with the central government over various issues in which they felt their sovereignty and their autonomy had been endangered.

In October, 1887 the provinces of Ontario, Quebec, Manitoba, Nova Scotia and New Brunswick held the first inter-provincial conference.

By the time the provincial premiers were through they had determined to remove from the federal government its power to veto provincial legislation, and to capture for themselves authority in all matters not specifically listed in the British North America Act as falling under federal jurisdiction. In all, there were 22 resolutions. In the face of this proposed mutiny by the provinces, the editor of the Montreal *Gazette* stated :

> It is not improbable that the people will, sooner than many now imagine, be called on to determine whether the work accomplished in 1867 is to be undone, whether the Confederation is to be preserved or allowed to lapse into its original fragments, preparatory to absorption in the United States ...

When he had led the movement towards Confederation in 1864 and '65, Macdonald had favoured a powerful central government and relatively feeble provincial governments. The American Civil War had just ended, and he blamed its outbreak on the nature of the American constitution. In drafting it, he said, the Americans had :

> ... commenced, in fact, at the wrong end. They declared by their constitution that each state was a sovereignty in itself, and the powers incident to a sovereignty belonged to each state, except those powers which, by the Constitution, were conferred upon the General Government and Congress. Here we have adopted a different system. We have strengthened the General Government.

> ... We have expressly declared that all subjects of general interest not distinctly and exclusively conferred upon the local governments ... shall be conferred upon the general government. We have thus avoided that great source of weakness which has been the cause of the disruption of the United States.

But in 1887, twenty years after Confederation, Macdonald found the provinces in revolt because they had been given too little power. Yet he feared the idea of increasing their power. For instance, there was the problem of the proposed enlargement of both the central provinces, Quebec and Ontario. He said :

> Now if you will look at the map and see the enormous extent of country proposed to be added to the two provinces, you will see what vast preponderance it gives them over the other provinces in the Dominion. History will repeat itself and posterity will find out that the evils that exist in other federations from the preponderance of one or more members will again happen. It is our duty as founders of a nation to look far into the future. I know it will be said that the additional territory desired by Ontario and Quebec is inhospitable in climate and ill-adapted for settlement, but we used to hear the same thing of the Red River country and the North-West. I have little doubt that the great portion of the vast region asked for by the two provinces will be capable of receiving and will receive a large population.

Macdonald feared that the two central provinces would become vast empires. Yet on all these problems he had to give in. The monopoly clause of the C.P.R. was abolished and Manitoba could therefore build railways wherever it chose to do so. The other provinces were pacified with better federal subsidies.

Macdonald was now getting on in years, but in the election of 1891, in which he saw as the main issue the continuance of the Imperial connection and the refusal of Canada to be absorbed into the United States, he demonstrated much vigor and zest. He was returned to office, but the election had taxed his health beyond the point of no return. Within three months of the election Macdonald was dead. His last few weeks have been movingly recorded by Macdonald's loyal private secretary, Joseph Pope :

On Tuesday, the 12th of May, I went over to his private rooms in the House of Commons as usual. About a quarter to four he came in, and went into the inner room, called me, and said that he was to meet his Excellency the Governor-General with Sir John Thompson at four o'clock. I noticed at the time that there was something wrong with his speech. I had had no experience of paralysis, but I felt sure this was a premonition of something serious. I came back to tell him Sir John Thompson would be there very soon. He said "He must come at once, because he must speak to the Governor for me, as I cannot talk. There is something the matter with my speech."

When the interview was over His Excellency and Sir John Thompson spoke to me privately on the subject, and both expressed their greatest concern, Lord Stanley saying he felt sure there was cause for alarm, as he had seen similar symptoms in the case of one who died of paralysis. After they left Sir John came into the outer office and spoke to me. For the first time in my life I noticed a trace of nervousness in his manner. "I am afraid of paralysis", he said; "both my parents died of it, and", he added slowly, "I seem to feel it creeping over me." I at once called a cab, and there being some delay, he and I walked down the Parliament grounds to meet it. He was then better, and got into the cab without difficulty. I begged him to let me drive home with him, but he would not permit it, saying, "There is no necessity." He added, "You must be careful not to mention this to Lady Macdonald."

Macdonald recovered sufficiently from this attack to pursue his official activities, and Pope even described him as being "like his old self" at times. However, sixteen days after the first attack, he had another. The report of his secretary, Joseph Pope, continues :

During the night, he suddenly called out of his sleep to Lady Macdonald, who immediately went to him, and found that his left arm was partially paralyzed. In the morning he was better, and the paralysis seemed to be wearing away. He appeared to feel the gravity of the situation, for he insisted on signing a certain document connected with the disposition of his property. I asked him when he wished to sign it. He said, "Now, while there is time." During the morning he instructed me to prepare for him two resolutions, of which he intended giving notice in the House of Commons. All that day he was much interested in public affairs, and his mind was as bright and active as ever.

On Friday morning, the 29th of May, he was the same as on the previous day, having passed a good night. About eleven o'clock he inquired, as he had done a hundred times before during slight indispositions, what letters there were. I answered that there were not many, and few of any importance, and asked if I should bring them up. He replied with a slight gesture of impatience, "Yes, of course." I did not bring them all up, however, but only a few of minor importance, to which he dictated some replies. I observed that he soon got tired, and I left the room about twelve.

About half-past two he sent for me about a trivial matter. When I left him he was reading the *North American Review,* and seemed easy in mind and body, so much so that the members of his family were encouraged to hope that the worst had passed. Indeed his composure might have deceived anyone unversed in medical science.

[While, from his expression of the day before, "I will sign now while there is time," as well as from what I afterwards learned that the doctors had told him,] there is little doubt that on that Friday afternoon Sir John fully realized the extreme gravity of his condition, yet neither by voice, look, nor manner did he manifest the slightest disquietude. The history of Sir John's last illness is in some respects an epitome of his life. As long as he could he strove against the sense of weariness that oppressed him, and when at length the inexorable laws of nature asserted their sway, he assumed that quiet dignity which ever marked his acceptance of the inevitable, and calmly awaited the last dread summons.

At half-past three the doctor called, and after spending a few minutes in the office, went upstairs. He sat down by the bedside, and put a few questions, which Sir John answered as usual.

About four o'clock, while conversing quietly with Dr. Powell, he gently leaned his head back on the pillow, yawned once or twice, and became apparently unconscious. The doctor at once saw that he had received a second stroke, this time complete right hemiplegia. From that moment, he never spoke nor exhibited more than a sort of semi-consciousness. He remained in this condition for eight days, passing quietly away at a quarter-past ten, on the evening of Saturday the 6th of June. The moment of his death was peaceful in the extreme. [In the afternoon the final change came.] His respiration, which had previously been very rapid, now became abnormally slow, and gradually slower and slower, until it ceased altogether.

The architect was no more. It fell to two French Canadians to announce his death to the nation and to pay their respects in the name of the Canadian nation and people. The first to speak was Sir Hector Langevin, who had been associated with Macdonald since the early days of the Liberal Conservative Party in the 1850s. In part Langevin said :

> Mr. Speaker, when the historians of Canada write the history of the last fifty years, they will have to write the life of Sir John A. Macdonald, and, in writing his life, they may not agree with all his public acts, but they cannot fail to say that he was a great man, a most distinguished stateman, and that his whole life was spent in the service of his country, dying in the midst of his official duty, not having had a day's rest before he passed to a better world. I need not express, Mr. Speaker, my own personal feelings. Having spent half of my life with him as his follower and as his friend, his departure is the same as if I lost half of my existence.
>
> I remember how devoted he was, not only to the old province of Canada, but how chivalrous he showed himself to the province of Quebec, and specially to my French-Canadian countrymen. [He had only to say a word, and, instead of being at the head of a small band of seventeen Upper Canada members, he would have had all the representatives of his province behind him. But, as he told me several times, he preferred to be just to his French compatriots and allies,] and the result was that, when Confederation came, the province of Quebec had confidence in him, and on his death-bed our great chief could see that his just policy had secured peace and happiness to all. Mr. Speaker, I should have wished to continue to speak of our dear departed friend, and spoken to you about his goodness of heart, the witness of which I have been so often, but I feel that I must stop; my heart is full of tears. I cannot proceed further."

Wilfrid Laurier, the Liberal leader, took up where Langevin had stopped :

> Mr. Speaker : I fully realize the emotion which chokes the honor- able gentleman. His silence, under the circumstances, is far more eloquent than any human language can be. I fully appreciate the intensity of the grief which fills the souls of all those who were the friends and followers of Sir John Macdonald, at the loss of the great leader whose whole life has been so closely identified with their party, a party upon which he has thrown such brilliancy and lustre. We on this side of the House, who were his opponents, who did not believe in his policy, nor in his methods of government — we take our full share of their grief — for the loss which they deplore today is far and away beyond and above the ordinary compass of party range. It is in every

THE APPRENTICESHIP

respect a great national loss, for he is no more who was, in many respects, Canada's most illustrious son, and in every sense Canada's foremost citizen and statesman.

Laurier concluded in the name of all :

Before the grave of him who, above all, was the father of Confederation, let not grief be barren grief; but let grief be coupled with the resolution, the determination, that the work in which Liberals and Conservatives, in which Brown and Macdonald united, shall not perish, but that though united Canada may be deprived of the services of her greatest men, still Canada shall and will live.

7

# ON THE BRINK OF RACIAL WARFARE
## The Manitoba School Question and the Election of 1896

In 1890 there occurred, in the frontier province of Manitoba, on the edge of the vast, almost uninhabited Canadian west, an event which rocked the 23-year-old nation to its foundations, and brought it to the brink of racial warfare.

The event was the Manitoba School Question. The Canadian humorist Stephen Leacock, who was intensely interested in his country's history, once wrote :

> The question was bitter in its intensity. The political life of Canada, then and today, moves on ground beneath which are the ashes of the fires of two centuries ago, of French against English, of Roman Catholic against Protestant. They can still be fanned to a flame; they might still precipitate a conflagration. Hence arises our ever-familiar warning to one another not to "raise the race cry". This to us is like "raising the devil" in the Middle Ages. *

The event which "raised the race cry" in 1890 was the passing, in the Manitoba legislature, of a bill abolishing the system of

* Stephen Leacock : *Canada — The Foundation of its Future,* 1941; commissioned and published by The House of Seagram, Ltd., Montreal. (Out of print).

separate Catholic and Protestant public schools in the province. Under the new legislation a uniform, non-denominational public school system was to be established.

This incident, although it was of immediate concern only to the residents of Manitoba, soon became a national issue. The "Manitoba School Question," as it came to be called, continued to be a national issue for six years. And by the end of that time it had helped to transform the political situation in Canada and to bring to power one of the greatest leaders the country has ever known.

To understand the Manitoba School Question, one must know something of the history of the province of Manitoba. This subject has been dealt with in detail in a previous program. Here is a summary of the main facts :

In 1870 the residents of that part of the Northwest Territories around what is now the city of Winnipeg, agreed to enter the three-year-old Canadian confederation as a province — to be called Manitoba — on several conditions. Among these were official recognition of the French language as well as English, and the granting of separate Protestant and Catholic schools. In the "List of Rights" presented to the Canadian government, the people of the Northwest demanded :

> ... that the schools be separate, and that the public money for schools be distributed among the different religious denominations in proportion to their respective populations according to the system in the Province of Quebec.

The residents of the Northwest insisted on these conditions because most of them — although they had intermarried with the Indians of the region — remained French-speaking and Catholic, and they feared that English-speaking Protestants would pour into "their" territory and outnumber them once their little corner of the Northwest had become a province of Canada. (Previously the Northwest had been owned and administered by the Hudson's Bay Company.)

The half-breeds of the Red River district — they were called Métis — had already staged an insurrection and shot one rabid

Protestant from Ontario when the Canadians started to conduct surveys in the Northwest.

So the Canadian government accepted the terms demanded, including the official recognition of French and the granting of separate schools.

Therefore, between 1871 and 1889 the Manitoba government had formed its dual school system, with separate administrations for the Roman Catholics and Protestants, and had ensured that financial support from public funds would be given to each system. That was — and is — the system in the province of Quebec. *

By 1890, however, the character of the population of Manitoba had altered considerably. Most of the immigrants who went there during the 20 years after Manitoba joined Confederation were Protestants and English-speaking. [The French-speaking Roman Catholics of the Red River District had been right in their predictions; they soon found themselves outnumbered and in danger of being assimilated.

During the first 20 years of Manitoba's history the Protestants had not agitated against the separate school system, but their opposition lay very near the surface and could easily be aroused. And it *was* aroused in 1888 when the premier of Quebec, Honoré Mercier, introduced his "Jesuit Estates Bill." This bill, discussed in an earlier program, made a financial settlement with the Jesuit order and certain agencies of the Church to compensate them for the land which had been taken away from the Jesuits when the British conquered New France in 1760. No one less than the Pope was to decide how the money was to be divided among the Jesuits and other ecclesiastical authorities. This kindled the anti-Catholic feelings of certain influential Protestants, who charged that a foreign power was being allowed to meddle in the business of a British dominion. Following as it did upon the Jesuit Estates affair, the Manitoba School Act of 1890 can be looked upon, partly, as an act of revenge.] The Protestants of Manitoba began to complain that

---

* After this script was written a Royal Commission on education in Quebec recommended the addition of neutral public schools to the Quebec school system. — K.M.

the dual system in their province was cumbersone and expensive, especially in the sparsely populated areas, and that it fostered religious and linguistic division where the aim should be unity and equality.

Encouragement, indeed leadership, in the Manitoba affair, came from Ontario, from Protestant groups such as the Orange Lodge, and especially from one D'Alton McCarthy, a fanatically anti-Catholic Member of Parliament. In a speech in Portage la Prairie, Manitoba, he told a cheering audience that the time had come :

> ... to make this a British country, in fact and in name. The separate school question in Manitoba and the Northwest, and the French school question in Ontario are local tasks which must be tackled first before the more difficult problems, that is, problems where vested interests are stronger, can be settled.

That was before the Manitoba legislature changed the education laws. Shortly afterwards the bill was passed, and the separate schools were no more. At the same session the legislature passed a law which abolished the official use of the French language in Manitoba. D'Alton McCarthy's work had been well done, and back in Ottawa, in another speech, he could say :

> ... The feeling was there. The grievance existed. Her people's mind had only to be directed to it, and the moment attention was drawn to it, the province of Manitoba rose as one man and said : "We want no dual language — and away with separate schools as well."

So much for the attitude of the Protestants, who were, for the moment at least, victorious. What about the Catholics ? The first significant action was taken by a Winnipeg physician, Dr. J.K. Barrett, a Catholic, who took the matter to court, challenging the right of the School District of Winnipeg to compel him to pay taxes for the support of the new non-denominational schools.

This case began the long and tortuous passage through the courts of the appeals and counter-appeals and counter-counter appeals which Stephen Leacock described as :

> ... about as interesting as a Privy Council decision on the sanitary authority of the City of London. *

---

* Leacock : *op cit*

That being so, we will not attempt to follow the case through the courts in any detail. Here is a brief summary of what happened :

1891 : two Manitoba Courts ruled that the Manitoba government was within its rights in passing the 1890 Manitoba School Act, abolishing separate schools.

Later the same year : the Supreme Court of Canada reversed the decision of the two Manitoba courts, saying that Manitoba legislation was unconstitutional.

June, 1892 : the Judicial Committee of the Privy Council of England reversed the decision of the Supreme Court of Canada, saying that the legislation by the Manitoba courts *was* constitutional.

After two years of litigation, the highest tribunal in the empire had ruled, and things were back where they had started. The Catholic minority's cause seemed doomed. During all this litigation the point at issue was that section of the Manitoba Act, under which Manitoba joined Confederation, which stated :

> ... No law on education made by the province should prejudicially affect any right or privilege with respect to denominational schools which any class of persons had by law or practice in the province at (the time of) the Union.

The Catholics of Manitoba argued that they had Catholic schools at the time of the union with Canada, and that they were therefore entitled to them after the union.

The courts argued that at the time of the union the Catholics possessed only the right to maintain *private* schools by gifts and fees, that they did not have the right to *tax-supported* Catholic schools.

Clearly the Catholics of Manitoba had lost the first round in the fight to maintain their separate schools. But they did not give up. Their next step was to apply to the Ottawa government for "remedial legislation" against the provincial government's act.

Both the British North America Act of 1867, which created the Dominion of Canada, and the Manitoba Act of 1870, which created the province of Manitoba and made it a part of Canada, provided for this "remedial legislation" against any act of the provincial government which violated the provisions respecting education:

[In case any such Provincial law as from time to time seems to the Governor-General in Council requisite for the due execution of the provisions of this section is not made, or in case any decision of the Governor-General in Council on any appeal under this section is not duly executed by the proper Provincial Authority in that behalf, then and in every such case, and as far only as the circumstances of each case require, the Parliament of Canada may make remedial laws for the due execution of the provisions of this section and of any decision of the Governor-General in Council under this section.]

In short, it was within the power of the federal government to change the Manitoba School Act if it believed that that act did an injustice to the Catholic minority. However, the federal government was reluctant to move. By over-riding the Manitoba government's original legislation to please the minority it would anger the majority — that is the Protestants — not only in Manitoba but in all of Canada. But if it did not do so, it would anger the Catholics everywhere — and these constituted the majority in the province of Quebec.

In order to evade having to make a decision, the government asked the Supreme Court of Canada whether it was empowered to take action on the Catholics' petition for "remedial action." A year later in February 1894, the Supreme Court said no. So the petitioners appealed that decision to the Judicial Committee of the Privy Council in England. Three years earlier this same court had said the Manitoba Government's new school act was constitutional. Obviously the Privy Council would not reverse its own decision. So it ruled that the federal government could "remedy" the situation as it saw fit to correct injustices, but without repealing the original legislation.

The judicial roundabout which had begun in 1890 was now ended. After five years of delay the federal government was now committed to action. On March 21st, 1895, the Cabinet issued a remedial order to Manitoba. The order stipulated the three fundamental rights of the minority which had been affected by the 1890 legislation :

- The right to establish public Roman Catholic Schools,
- The right to share proportionately any subsidies made by the provincial government in aid of education, and
- The right to be excused from having to support the public school system if rate payers supported the Roman Catholic schools.

The federal government first attempted to persuade the Manitoba government to correct these abuses by amending its own legislation, but the Manitoba government refused. So, in the speech from the Throne, opening the 1896 session of the federal parliament, the Conservative government announced, reluctantly, that remedial legislation would be introduced.

The remedial act, introduced a month later, provided for a separate Catholic school board which would appoint teachers and inspectors with the qualifications specified by the Manitoba Department of Education. Roman Catholics would be able to elect to pay their municipal school tax to support their school, and those who did so would be exempt from paying taxes for the public school system.

The act had many weaknesses — which would be thrashed out in the debate which would follow in parliament. However, it was acceptable to the religious authorities. Archbishop Langevin of St. Boniface, Manitoba, telegraphed dramatically :

> Lex applicabilis efficax et satisfactoria. Probo illam. Omnes episcopi et veri catholici approbare debent. Vita in lege.

In other words, the episcopacy accepted fully the remedial bill. The Rev. Father Albert Lacombe, a pioneer western missionary whom everyone honoured and respected, sent an open letter to Wilfrid Laurier, leader of the opposition Liberal Party, urging the him to support the Conservative government's remedial bill.

> My Dear Sir :
> In this critical time in the question of the Manitoba Schools, permit an aged missionary, today representing the Bishops of your country in this cause which concerns us all, permit me to appeal

to your faith, your patriotism, and to your spirit of justice, to entreat you to accede to our request. It is in the name of our Bishops, of the hierarchy and the Catholics of Canada, that we ask the party of which you are the very worthy chief, to assist us in settling this famous question and to do so by voting with the government on the remedial bill. [We do not ask you to vote for the government, but for the bill which will render us our rights, the bill which will be presented to the House in a few days.

I consider — or rather we all consider — that such an act of courage, goodwill, and sincerity on your part and from those who follow your policy will be greatly in the interest of your party, especially in the general elections.

I must tell you that we cannot accept your commission of inquiry on any account and shall do our best to fight it.]

If, may God not grant, you do not believe it to be your duty to accede to our just demands and if the government which is anxious to give us just and honest law is beaten, and overthrown while keeping firm to the end of the struggle, I inform you with regret that the episcopacy, like one man, united with the clergy, will rise to support those who may have fallen in defending us.

Please pardon the frankness which leads me to speak thus; though I am not your intimate friend, still I may say that we have been on good terms. Always I have deemed you a gentleman, a respectable citizen, and a man well fitted to be at the head of a political party. May divine providence keep up your courage and your energy for the good of our common country.

I remain sincerely and respectfully, honoured sir, your most humble and devoted servant.

Albert Lacombe, O.M.I.

This was clearly an ultimatum, but on March 3, 1896, Laurier rose in the House of Commons to announce his party's policy regarding the Manitoba school crisis. It was clear that the church was not going to pressure him into following anything but the dictates of his own conscience :

Mr. Speaker ... in the course of my parliamentary career never did I rise, Sir, with a greater sense of security, never did I feel so strong in the consciousness of right as I do now at this anxious moment, when in the name of a constitution so outrageously misinterpreted by the government in the name of peace and harmony in this land, when in the name of the minority which this Bill seeks or pretends to help, when in the name of this young nation, on which so many hopes are centred. I rise to ask Parliament not to proceed any further with this Bill.

Laurier argued that the powers of control which the federal government had over the provinces could only be exercised with moderation and only in such a way as to avoid irritation. The government having bungled from the beginning, he said, it was impossible to allow it to continue to bungle, especially since it would mean the alienation of the Province of Manitoba. Without the Province of Manitoba's cooperation, there could be no settlement of the school question. Laurier continued :

[There are men in this House who are against separate schools, but who would have no objection to the re-establishment of separate schools in Manitoba, provided they were re-established by the province of Manitoba itself. There are men in this House who are not in favour of separate schools, but who think very strongly that it would not be advisable to interfere with the legislation of Manitoba at all until all means of conciliation had been exhausted. Sir, in face of this perilous position, I maintain today, and I submit it to the consideration of gentlemen on both sides, that the policy of the Opposition, affirmed since many years, reiterated on more than one occasion, is the only policy which can successfully deal with this question — the only policy which can remedy the grievance of the minority, while at the same time not violently assaulting the right of the majority and thereby perhaps creating a greater wrong. This was the policy which, for my part, I adopted and developed the very first time the question came before this House, and upon this policy today I stand once more.

Sir, I cannot forget at this moment that the policy which I have advocated and maintained all along has not been favourably received in all quarters.] Not many weeks ago I was told from high quarters in the Church to which I belong that unless I supported the school bill which was then being prepared by the government and which we now have before us, I would incur the hostility of a great and powerful body. Sir, this is too grave a phase of this question for me to pass over in silence.

[I have only this to say : even though I have threats over me, coming as I am told, from high dignitaries in the Church to which I belong, no word of bitterness shall ever pass my lips as against that Church. I respect it and I love it. Sir, I am not of that school which has long been dominant in France and other countries of continental Europe, which refuses ecclesiastics the right of a voice in public affairs. No, I am a liberal of the English school. I believe in that school which has all along claimed that it is the privilege of all subjects, whether high or low, whether rich or poor, whether ecclesiastic or laymen, to participate in the administration of public affairs, to discuss, to influence, to persuade, to convince — but which has always denied even to the highest the right to dictate — even to the lowest.]

I am here representing not Roman Catholics alone but Protestants as well, and I must give an account of my stewardship to all classes. [Here am I, a Roman Catholic of French extraction, entrusted by the confidence of the men who sit around me with great and important duties under our constitutional system of government.] I am here the acknowledged leader of a great party, composed of Roman Catholics and Protestants as well [as Protestants must be in the majority in every party in Canada]. Am I to be told, I, occupying such a position, that I am to be dictated the course I am to take in this House, by reasons that can appeal to the consciences of my fellow-Catholic members, but which do not appeal as well to the consciences of my Protestant colleagues ? No. So long as I have a seat in this House, so long as I occupy the position I do now, whenever it shall become my duty to take a stand upon any question whatever, that stand I will take not upon grounds of Roman Catholicism, not upon grounds of Protestantism, but upon grounds which can appeal to the conscience of all men, irrespective of their particular faith, upon grounds which can be occupied by all men who love justice, freedom and toleration.

[So far as this Bill is concerned, I have given you my views.]

The government's bill was not destined to become law. The legal life of Parliament expired before it could be passed, and the Manitoba School Question became the main issue in the general election of 1896.

Between the proroguing of parliament and the general election, the Conservative Party reorganized itself in preparation for the fight ahead. McKenzie Bowell, who had served as prime minister since the death of Sir John Thomson in 1894, was replaced by Sir Charles Tupper as head of the party. The French-Canadian contingent in the party was strengthened, and more ultra-conservatives were put in positions of importance.

The electoral campaign which followed was fought bitterly. The key province was, of course, Quebec, and it was here that Laurier's main fight against Sir Charles Tupper was waged. Not only had the Conservatives won elections steadily in Quebec since 1878; now they could represent themselves as guardians of the rights of French-Canadians in other parts of Canada, because of their remedial bill in the Manitoba School Question.

Naturally the bishops and the clergy were in open sympathy with the Conservatives. The bishops were preparing their "mandement", that is, an episcopal letter to instruct French-Canadians in meeting electoral responsibilities.

Bishop Langevin explained that the bishops accepted the Conservative government's bill because :

> The remedial legislation consecrates the principle of separate schools, and that for eternity. This principle is too essential and too precious to me to allow me to reject it even though the financial provisions of the remedial legislation are not wholly satisfactory.

The other bishops rallied behind Bishop Langevin and accepted the bill. Only the Archbishop of Montreal and the Bishop of Valleyfield had serious reservations about it and it was largely because of them that no collective episcopal mandement was ever issued which accepted the remedial legislation unreservedly. However, on May 16, 1896, the bishops did make public their episcopal letter in which they declared themselves the natural judges of the question. They said they did not wish to "descend into the political arena" but they concluded the mandement by insisting :

> ... That all Catholics should vote only for candidates who will personally and solemnly pledge themselves to vote in Parliament in favour of the legislation giving to the Catholics of Manitoba the school laws which were recognized as theirs by the Privy Council of England.

In many parishes priests made sure that their parishioners understood the intimate thoughts of the bishops. This clerical intervention assisted the Conservatives, who used the episcopal letter to demonstrate that the Church was solidly behind them in their efforts to solve the Manitoba School Crisis.
Furthermore, all but one of the Quebec bishops insisted on written declarations from all the candidates, pledging themselves to uphold the rights of the Manitoba Catholics. Every candidate in Quebec, except eight Liberals, signed the pledge.

In Trois Rivières, the old and impetuous Bishop La Fleche ignored the episcopal order not to comment on the mandement. In a sermon he referred to this passage from Laurier's famous speech :

> So long as I have a seat in this House, so long as I occupy the
> position I do now, whenever it shall become my duty to take a
> stand upon any question whatever, that stand I will take not upon
> grounds of Roman Catholicism, nor upon grounds of Protestantism,
> but upon grounds which can appeal to the consciences of all men,
> irrespective of their particular faith, upon grounds which can be
> occupied by all men who love justice, freedom and toleration.

This, Bishop La Fleche said, was :

> The most categorical affirmation of the liberalism condemned by
> the Church which has ever been made, to my knowledge, in any
> assembly of our country. The man who speaks thus is a rationalist
> liberal. He formulates a doctrine entirely opposed to the Catholic
> doctrine; that is to say, that a Catholic is not bound to be a
> Catholic in his public life ... Under the circumstances a Catholic
> cannot under pain of sinning in a grave manner vote for the chief
> of a party who has formulated so publicly such an error.

[It was this sermon which inspired a curé to tell his parishioners
to :

> Choose the bishop or Barabbas Laurier !

In Ontario the bishops made no pronouncement, and in the
Maritimes the only exception was the Bishop of Antigonish,
who declared that after careful study of the Holy Gospels and
the party platforms he was :

> ... officially in a position to declare, and I hereby declare, that
> it is the plain conscientious duty of every Catholic elector to vote
> for the Conservative candidate, and this declaration no Catholic in
> this diocese, be he priest or layman, has a right to dispute.]

The Liberals answered such attacks, but it was not in arguing
with bishops that they hoped to win the election of 1896.
The Liberal party, under its Quebec organizer-in-chief, Joseph
Israel Tarte, had been preparing for the election of 1896 ever
since the beginning of the Manitoba School Crisis. Tarte, like
many others, believed that the Manitoba school legislation and
the ordinances which had ended the official use of the French
language in the Northwest, were manifestations of racial and
religious discrimination which the Conservative party had not
been able to prevent or to remedy. Tarte proposed to unite
the French-Canadian minority under the Liberal banner of
Laurier. So united, the French Canadians would be powerful
enough to demand their rights.

By the time the federal election arrived, in June 1896, the Quebec Liberal party had been completely refashioned. The candidates had been chosen with great care to ensure that most of them would be acceptable even to Conservative voters. Party literature had been distributed widely and Laurier's name was now known to all, and thousands of his countrymen had met him.

A month before the election Tarte wrote to the editor of the Toronto *Globe* that he was confident of a Liberal victory in the province of Quebec.

Tarte was right. On June 23, the people of Quebec ignoring the warnings of the Church, elected 49 Liberals to Parliament, and only 16 Conservatives. Ontario voters also favoured the Liberal candidates, as did those in the Territories and British Columbia. In the Maritimes the Liberals and Conservatives came out even. Paradoxically, only in Manitoba — the province which the Conservative government was supposed to be coercing — were the Conservatives victorious.

A desire for change, impatience over the government's handling of the Manitoba School Question, dissatisfaction with its fiscal policy, and lack of strong leadership since the death of Sir John A. Macdonald : these were among the reasons given for the "calamity", as Archbishop Langevin called the Conservative defeat.

Since 1878 the Conservative party had reigned supreme. Now, from 1896 to 1911 the Liberal party was to govern. The Liberal victory marked the end of one era in Canadian politics and the beginning of another. For the first time the Canadian confederation was to be led by a French Canadian. Everywhere the moderate elements were allied to one another in one party dedicated to tolerance, moderation and compromise.

It was, for example, in a spirit of compromise that the Manitoba School Question was finally resolved after 1896, in negotiations between the province and the federal government. Separate schools were not restored, but provision was made for denominational religious instruction where there was a demand for it, and for instruction in French where there were enough French-Canadian students to justify it. This compromise satisfied the province and Protestant leaders. But Quebec bishops were furious over :

> ... this indefensible abandonment of the best established and most sacred rights of the Catholic minority,

and it would be a long time before the church hierarchy could accept Laurier and Liberalism.

The political influence of the bishops and the clergy, though still a force to be reckoned with in French Canada, would never be used so openly again. French-Canadians in the province of Quebec, and elsewhere, had decided that, in political matters, they could make their own decisions.

A new era had begun in the history of Canada.

# "A PILLAR OF FIRE"                                        8
## Two Types of
## French-Canadian Nationalism

One of the main aims of the French-Canadian nationalist movement has been to press for equitable treatment of the French-speaking minority of Canada. It has been a protest movement against English-speaking Canadians who have never been too willing to grant to the French-speaking minorities in their provinces the rights and privileges which the English-speaking minority enjoys in the province of Quebec.

In the period with which this program is concerned, from 1896 (when Wilfrid Laurier became prime minister) to the First World War, another aspect of French-Canadian nationalism came to the fore : a protest against British imperialism. French-Canadians feared that Canada's manpower and resources would be depleted to protect an empire which awoke in their hearts no sentiment of loyalty or love. They insisted that Canadians belonged at home, not off in South Africa during the Boer War, or in the trenches of France during the First World War.

Their first loyalty was to Canada, and their first responsibility was to develop its resources and to achieve its autonomy. One French-Canadian nationalist once stated :

> The stronger Canada grows in population and wealth, the slighter will be the dangers that may threaten her security, and the greater her contribution to the welfare and glory of the Empire. Therefore the best way in which a Canadian, be he French-speaking or English-speaking, can play his part in the building up of the Empire is not by diverting the healthiest and strongest portion of its population from the pursuits of a peaceful and industrious life and sending them to fight in all parts of the world. We must not foster in Canada the spirit of militarism. Canada will be an attractive and prosperous country only if she is kept aloof from all military adventures.

When England conquered New France in 1760, it inherited a people who possessed all the characteristics of a nation, except independence. The French of the New World were as different from those of the mother country as the Americans were different from the English at the time of the American Revolution. And they thought of themselves as constituting a nation.

Attempts were made to reconcile this "nation" into the bosom of a single state, but they had not been too successful. Even Confederation did not achieve much success in this regard. One has only to remember the revolts of the French-speaking Métis of the west, under Louis Riel, the fight for separate schools in Manitoba, and other matters discussed in earlier programs to grasp this essential fact of Canadian history. Disappointed over their lot within Canada, the French Canadians tended more and more to regard Quebec as their homeland. In this process French Canadians became more and more isolated. The extreme ones viewed their English-speaking compatriots as imperialist war-mongers who were willing to hurl Canada into military madness. On the other hand English-speaking Canadians viewed their French-speaking counterparts as cowards and as a reactionary force which had to be crushed in order to assure the maintenance of British supremacy over the Canadian part of the North American continent.

Not only was there a gulf separating English and French Canadians because of their different aims and attitudes, but the French Canadians were also divided among themselves. This division can best be seen in a study of the two French Canadian leaders who emerged to fight the battle for their people during the last years of the nineteenth century and the first decades of the twentieth.

One was old, moderate, a staunch Liberal, a follower of Gladstone, a man who for fifteen years assured a strong and vigorous leadership in Canadian development as prime minister of his country. This was Wilfrid Laurier.

The other, equally brilliant, was younger, more violent, an extremist by nature, a leader by temperament, a powerful and logical politician. This was Henri Bourassa.

On the shoulders of these two men rested, to a large extent, the destiny of Canada at the turn of this century.

Henri Bourassa became the leader of the French-Canadian extreme nationalist movement after 1899 when he resigned from Laurier's Liberal party — in protest over Canada's participation in the Boer War. He admitted that he had duties toward Great Britain, but insisted that these duties were limited to "fidelity to the British Crown", by which he meant the maintenance of the monarchical character of Canada. He believed that French Canadians had done enough for England. They had maintained British supremacy in America during the American Revolution, and they had helped to keep Canada British during the War of 1812 against the United States. The French Canadian debt had therefore been paid. No new accounts were to be opened, for as he said :

> The Canadian people has done in the past more than its duty to assure the maintenance of English power in America. The Canadian people now refuses to impose upon itself new sacrifices for the organization and defence of the Empire, and affirms that the duty of the colonies in this respect is limited to the defense of their respective territories.

But were French Canadians part of the Canadian people? Bourassa had no doubt about that. They were the equal partners in the gigantic adventure that was Canada:

> The nation that we wish to see develop is the Canadian nation, composed of French Canadians and English Canadians, that is of two elements separated by language and religion, and by the legal dispositions necessary for the preservation of their respective traditions, but united in a feeling of brotherhood, in a common attachment to the common fatherland.

If Bourassa thought that way, why did he appeal to French-Canadian particularism? Bourassa once answered this question by replying:

> I appeal to my race in order that, conscious of its dignity, it may stand up straight and proud before others, not as an enemy but to accept their hands. I appeal to my race in order that in the province of Quebec there shall be no more question of popular passions, but only of honour and dignity, and in order that I may prove to our sister provinces that if we have remained at home, alone, without having perhaps as much wealth as others, the little that we have has sufficed to keep us honest, and worthy of those who have preceded us. I appeal to my race in order that it may understand that we are united, Catholics and French, English and Protestants, not to fight and crush each other, but to work with a common mind to enlarge our country.

A good summary of Bourassa's nationalist views appeared in a series of articles which he wrote for *Le Devoir,* the Montreal newspaper he founded. The series was entitled: "Why Annexation is no more dreaded by French Canadians". He began by stating:

> In this short study, I do not intend to express mere nationalist thoughts or feelings, but to define as impartially as possible the various opinions that are beginning to shape themselves in many French-Canadian minds, their growing instincts and tendencies, and the results that may accrue therefrom.

> French Canadians have been the staunchest and most constant opponents of annexation to the United States. This is now a truism in history. At a time when they held in their hands the fate of the Colony, they refused to join hands with the rebels in the English colonies; they resisted the appeals of Lafayette and of France herself; they shed their blood for the defence of the British flag and institutions. Later on, they persistently opposed all annexationist movements and every fiscal or administrative policy capable of strengthening the centripetal force of the great American

Republic. But they are beginning to doubt the utility of their efforts. Especially they ask themselves what they have gained by their constant loyalty to the British Crown and their unswerving devotion to the unity of Canada. In vain they look for evidences of gratitude on the part of their fellow-citizens of British origin, who have worked neither as long nor as hard as they for the building up of the common country, in the benefits of which Anglo-Canadians seem now to claim the larger share.

Bourassa then went on to ask questions which French Canadians have always asked :

Where does he find himself one hundred and forty years after his defense of Quebec against Arnold and Montgomery, one hundred years after the Battle of Chateauguay, seventy years after the unjust provisions of the Union Act of 1841 ? Above all, where is he forty-five years after the birth of the Federal regime, offered to him as a remedy to all his grievances and the solution of the racial problem — that regime which, after twenty-five years of existence, was defined by its principle framer, Sir John A. Macdonald, as having established "absolute equality of rights" between both races, in matters "of language and religion, of property and of persons" ?

Bourassa then answered his own question :

It has all ended in his being told that, in law and in fact, his rights are confined to the Province of Quebec, as those of the Indians to their reserves. His language, one of the two official idioms of the country, is excluded from teaching in nearly all the public schools for the support of which he pays his taxes. He is now threatened with a still closer restriction of the very meagre place given to the French language in its own separate and bi-lingual schools in Ontario. The extraordinary efforts to which he is forced, in order to secure a partial usage of that same language in all the public utilities organised by the various legislatures of his country, and subsidised from the public chest in which his share of contribution falls constantly, are qualified and denounced as rebellious and demagogic.

Bourassa then proceeded to blast English-speaking indifference :

But what is still more characteristic, is the hostility or indifference shown by most English-speaking Canadians of all classes, toward the maternal language of one-fourth of their fellow-citizens, who constitute the most ancient group of the population of Canada — that group which has undergone the heaviest sacrifices for the maintenance of Canadian unity and the preservation of the rights of the British Crown in America.

Harvard University, in the United States, does more for high French culture than all of the English-speaking universities of

Canada, with the exception of McGill. French is more frequently heard, and better spoken, in well-educated circles of Boston, New York or Washington, than in Toronto, or even the English-speaking sets of Montreal, in population the fifth French centre of the world, in the very heart of this province of Quebec, where the Anglo-Protestant minority enjoys the most privileged situation ever granted to a religious or national minority.

Inspired by Bourassa, and provoked by certain incidents, a vast and aggressive new nationalist movement was born. The incidents included the sending of Canadian troops to fight alongside British troops in the Boer war, the refusal of English-speaking Canada to recognize fully the French language and French schools in the new provinces of Saskatchewan and Alberta, and the curtailment of the use of the French language in the separate schools of Ontario.

The reaction of the nationalistic French Canadians to these provocations could be seen in their literature, in the labour movement (with the development of national unions as rivals to the international English-speaking unions), and in economics, as the new nationalists fought vehemently the development of Quebec's natural resources by English and American capital.

The younger generation became more and more intent upon stressing its Frenchness and Catholicity, and came to regard all English institutions as wrong.

Through the founding of so-called Catholic Action groups, which were more devoted to fostering nationalist sentiments than to fostering the Kingdom of Christ on earth; through the fact that the clergy was devoted to the French cause and that almost all education lay in their hands; and through the bitter disappointment caused by constant rebuffs across the country, a generation of French Canadians developed a narrow provincialism and withdrew within the shell of an exclusive and isolated French and Catholic province.

---

Henri Bourassa's rival for the leadership of the French-Canadian people was Wilfrid Laurier, leader of the Liberal Party from 1887 and Prime Minister of Canada from 1896 until 1911.

Laurier combined with his love for his country, his language and his ancestry, a deep respect for British institutions and a willing recognition of the duties and responsibilities of British subjects. It was on this matter that Bourassa parted company with Laurier, under whom he had served in the Liberal party and the Canadian government in Ottawa. Bourassa could not accept the sending of Canadian troops to fight in the Boer War. Laurier, on the other hand, spoke of "the beneficial results which will accrue from that action."

Laurier spent most of his life vindicating Quebec to the rest of Canada and explaining the attitudes of English Canada to Quebec. He himself described his life's aim as being :

> To promote unity and harmony and amity between the diverse elements of this country.

To Laurier, every incident, potentially divisive as it may have been, had to be seen as an instrument to promote unity. For instance, in sending Canadian troops to South Africa he reminded Bourassa and the Canadian people :

> [My honourable friend reads the consequences of this action in sending out a military contingent to South Africa.] Let me tell you from the bottom of my heart that my heart is full of the hopes I entertain of the beneficial results which will accrue from that action. When our young volunteers sailed from our shores to join the British army in South Africa, great were our expections that they would display on those distant battle-fields the same courage which had been displayed by their fathers when fighting against one another in the last century. Again, in many breasts there was a fugitive sense of uneasiness at the thought that the first facing of musketry by raw recruits is always a severe trial. But when the telegraph brought us the news that such was the good impression made by our volunteers that the Commander-in-Chief had placed them in the post of honour, in the first rank, to share the danger with that famous corps, the Gordon Highlanders; when we heard that they had justified fully the confidence placed in them, that they had charged like veterans, that their conduct was heroic and had won for them the encomiums of the Commander-in-Chief and the unstinted admiration of their comrades, who had faced death upon a hundred battle-fields in all parts of the world — is there a man whose bosom did not swell with pride — the pride of pure patriotism, the pride of consciousness of our rising strength, the pride of consciousness that that day it had been revealed to the world that a new power had arisen in the West ?

Nor is that all. The work of union and harmony between the chief races of this country is not yet complete. But there is no bond of union so strong as the bond created by common dangers faced in common. Today there are men in South Africa representing the two branches of the Canadian family, fighting side by side for the honour of Canada. Already some of them have fallen, giving to their country the last full measure of devotion. Their remains have been laid in the same grave, there to rest to the end of time in the last fraternal embrace. Can we not hope — I ask my honourable friend himself — that in that grave shall be buried the last vestiges of our former antagonism? If such shall be the result, if we can indulge that hope, if we can believe that in that grave shall be buried the former contentions, the sending of the contingents would be the greatest service ever rendered to Canada since Confederation.

Often Laurier made his profession of faith :

I am a Canadian. Canada has been the inspiration of my life. I have had before me as a pillar of fire by night and a pillar of cloud by day a policy of true Canadianism, of moderation, of conciliation... In all the difficulties, all the pains, and all the vicissitudes of our situation, let us always remember that love is better than hatred, and faith better than doubt, and let hope in our future destinies be the pillar of fire to guide us in our career.

Laurier never ceased to battle what he felt his rival, Henri Bourassa, represented. He referred to him and to his allies as :

...the Pharisee end of Canadian Catholicism. They have constituted themselves the defenders of a religion which no one attacked; those who handle the holy water sprinkler as if it were a club; those who have arrogated to themselves the monopoly of orthodoxy; [those who excommunicate right and left all whose stature is a little greater than theirs;] those who seem to have only hatred and envy for their motives and instinct... [those, originally, whom the people with their picturesque language designated under the name of Castors, Beavers.]

Laurier appealed to a broader nationalism. On one occasion, he said :

We are French-Canadians, but our country is not confined to the territory overshadowed by the citadel of Quebec; our country is Canada, it is all that is covered by the British flag on the American continent... Our fellow-countrymen are not only those in whose veins runs the blood of France. They are all those, whatever their race or whatever their language, whom the fortune of war, the chances of fate or their own choice have brought among us and who acknowledge the sovereignty of the British Crown...

The rights of my fellow-countrymen of different origins are as dear to me, as sacred to me, as the rights of my own race... What I claim for ourselves is an equal place in the sun, an equal share of justice, of liberty; that share we have; we have it amply and what we claim for ourselves we are anxious to grant to others. [I am not ignorant of the fact that there can be no nation without a national pride, nor am I unaware that in almost all cases national pride is inspired by those tragic events which bring suffering and tears in their train, but which at the same time call out all the forces of a nation or of a race... Our history under Confederation presents none of the dramatic events which make us so attached to the past; it has been calm and consequently happy. But peace has also its glories and its heroes.]

Then, significantly, Sir Wilfrid chose to give as examples of great Canadians two English-speaking statesmen, Sir John A. Macdonald, the first prime minister and later the leader of the opposition Conservative party, and Edward Blake, the leader of the English wing of his own party.

The first name I shall recall is that of a man from whom I differ *toto caelo*, but I am too much a French-Canadian not to glory at all times in doing justice to an adversary. I refer to Sir John Macdonald. I will not astonish my friend, Mr. Chapais, whom I see among us, if I state that I do not share Sir John Macdonald's political opinions. I may even add that I condemn almost all of them, but it must be acknowledged that in his long career Sir John Macdonald has displayed such eminent qualities that he would have made his mark on any of the world's stages, and that with the single exception perhaps of Mr. Mercier, no one on this continent has excelled as he has in the art of governing men. The other name is that of a man who has been to me not only a friend, but more than a friend, — I mean Hon. Edward Blake. Some years ago, speaking here of Mr. Blake, I declared that in my opinion America did not possess his equal and Europe could not show his superior. That opinion has been confirmed by all I have since seen of Mr. Blake. I have enjoyed the advantage of very close relations with him, and have learned that is heart, soul and character are in keeping with his splendid intellect...

Bourassa would perhaps never have considered that two English-speaking Canadians who could not speak French were examples of great Canadians. Nevertheless, like Laurier, Bourassa believed that for Canada to endure, French-speaking Canadians and English-speaking Canadians would have to form a dynamic partnership. Bourassa tended to be more intransigent and appeared to be unable to realize that the attainment of that ideal would take time. Laurier, on the other hand, was more moderate and believed that time could erase the difficulties of the present if men displayed good will, understanding and tolerance. He laboured under no delusion that these qualities were present in the Canadian state. But, as a builder of a nation, he had to have faith in the possibility of their attainment. It is because of such faith and dreams and hope that the Canadian entity has endured.

# A HOUSE IN GOOD ORDER 9
## The Work of Sir Wilfrid Laurier

The Liberal Party's victory over the Conservatives in the federal election of 1896 coincided with the end of a world-wide recession which had hindered the economic development of the new nation for two decades — that is, almost from its beginning.

Industrial development in Europe increased, and this was accompanied by a rapid growth in urbanization, which increased the demand for foodstuffs. Canada, mainly an agricultural nation, benefitted from the increased demand for food — and from its increased value, and the vast Canadian prairies were thus able to compete in the international market. But more people were needed to exploit the resources of the prairies profitably, and the new Prime Minister, Wilfrid Laurier, therefore embarked upon a policy of rapid immigration. During Laurier's regime — from 1896 to 1911, a million people moved into what are now the three prairie provinces of Manitoba, Saskatchewan and Alberta, and the production of wheat increased from 29 million bushels to 209 million bushels.

In the midst of this prosperity, Wilfrid Laurier pursued roughly the same policies that John A. Macdonald had pursued before him. Laurier's policy, like Macdonald's, consisted of some protection to Canadian industries, the building of an effective transportation system, and the settlement of the west.

But Laurier was more fortunate than Macdonald. For not only had the world's economic situation improved by the time he took office, but the agricultural areas of the western United States had become filled, and the United States' agricultural surpluses were being reduced by internal consumption. Now it was Canada's turn to attract immigrants and foreign capital.

The period 1896 to 1911 in Canada was a boom period, and the American concept of "manifest destiny" had its counterpart in Canada in Laurier's slogan "The twentieth century will be Canada's".

The economic policies of the Liberal party had been drafted at the convention of 1893 — three years before the Liberals came to power. At that time, Wilfrid Laurier had declared :

> Let it be well understood that from this moment we have a distinct issue with the party in power. Their ideal is protection, our ideal is free trade. Their immediate object is protection; ours a tariff for revenue only. Upon this issue we engage the battle from this moment forward, and I ask you once more never to desist until we have achieved victory, until we have freed this country from the incubus which has been weighing it down for fifteen long years.

This anti-protectionist policy became one of the most important planks of the Liberal platform during the election of 1896. But it is difficult to determine whether it had much to do with the Liberal victory. Possibly more significant was the fact that Conservative party was disorganized and had seen constant changes of leadership since the death of Sir John A. Macdonald, Canada's first prime minister, five years earlier. The Manitoba School Question, discussed in an earlier program, had raised a racial and religious issue which the Conservatives had permitted to go unresolved for almost six years. And political immorality had been uncovered in high places, some of it involving ministers of the Crown.

In any case, no one could be sure that the Liberal party was really wholeheartedly dedicated to free trade. Laurier's party included eminent protectionists, and Laurier himself, later in the convention speech we have just heard, qualified his first, "pro free trade" remarks :

> Nothing is more difficult — and that is one of the evils of protection — than to wipe away protection, because under it interests have been established which every man who has at heart the interest of all classes must take into consideration. It is always easy to increase the tariff, because by so doing you increase the private fortunes of certain individuals. But whenever you decrease the tariff it has always to be done with careful consideration, and I am sure that when the Liberals are in power they will not be indifferent to this primary truth.

By admitting that the road to free trade would be a long one, and that they were in favour of a tariff for revenue, the Liberals were provided with a great degree of flexibility in the manipulation of the tariff rate. In presenting his first budget, the finance minister, W.S. Fielding, insisted that a rapid removal of tariff protection would, in the long run, mean a dislocation of Canadian economic life. Moreover, the minister argued that the tariff situation in the United States had changed considerably with the arrival of a Republican president.

Consequently, it was imperative for the Canadians to go slowly until it was known whether the American trend towards protectionism would continue. The Liberal administration was in no doubt as to what must be done if the Americans were hostile to the Canadians in their commercial policy. As the finance minister stated :

> We must be prepared to deal with this question from the point of view of having one tariff for the countries which are willing to trade with us, and a different tariff for the countries which are not.

As a result of their displeasure with the United States' protectionist policy, the Canadian government — headed by a French Canadian — decided that the time had come to grant some form of preference to Imperial trade. This had been talked about for a long time, but nothing had ever been done about it. Laurier was able to arrange for preferential treatment, and

THE APPRENTICESHIP

the reasoning behind this policy was enunciated by the Minister of Finance, in his first budget speech of 1897 :

> Why should we wait for England to take action ? England has dealt generously with us in the past. England has given us a larger degree of liberty perhaps than is possessed by any country on the face of the earth. She has given us liberty to tax her even when she admits our goods free. And we have taxed them to an enormous degree. Why should we wait for England to do more ? Somebody must make a move in this matter and we propose that Canada should lead the way.

Fielding's tariff of 1897 did not destroy the edifice of protection created by the Conservatives in an earlier era. The new Government attempted to satisfy everyone. It established a general tariff to protect Canadian industries, and it offered some solace to the free-trader by offering a special adjustment in the tariffs for any country which treated Canada as a favoured nation.

This remained by and large the Liberal policy until the defeat of the Government over the question of free trade, or "reciprocity", with the United States in 1911.

But the economic boom of the late 1890's and of the first decade of the 20th Century did not depend only upon protection to Canadian industries. It also depended on the settlement of the West. This, in many ways, is the basic achievement of the Liberal party between 1896 and 1911. The glory for capitalizing on the world situation by bringing settlers to the West must be given to Clifford Sifton, the Minister of the Interior in the first three administrations headed by Wilfrid Laurier. Sifton's agent travelled the length and breadth of Europe, attracting immigrants. In addition, many in Eastern Canada left their homes to settle in the West, encouraged by the Government's land policy. For instance, every person emigrating to the West could obtain a free homestead of 160 acres or could buy 640 acres very cheaply. The Canadian Pacific Railway and the Hudson's Bay Company, which had millions of acres, cooperated extensively in this gigantic undertaking. The immigrants who invaded the West were industrious and bent on success. Railway lines flourished, towns grew up, roads spread, and the great natural and business possibilities of the West were exploited. Wilfrid Laurier has left one of the clearest statements ever made by anyone on the place which the prairies occupied in the Canadian economy :

> Settlers in Western Canada will require clothes, they will require furniture, they will require implements, they will require shoes — and I hope you can furnish them in Quebec — they will require everything that man has to be supplied with. It is your ambition, it is my ambition also, that this scientific tariff of ours will make it possible that every shoe that has to be worn in those Prairies shall be a Canadian shoe; that every yard of cloth that can be marketed there shall be a yard of cloth produced in Canada; [and so on, and so on.]

In 1905 the provinces of Alberta and Saskatchewan, formerly part of the Northwest Territories, were created by Acts of Parliament. There was an unpleasant moment about separate schools on which the Liberal party almost perished and which cost it the support of many important men, including Clifford Sifton. This unpleasant moment also raised once again the cry of 'race', since religion cannot be discussed in Canada without attracting it. The Conservatives were in favour of leaving the matter of education to the provinces, while, on the other hand, the French Canadians and the Roman Catholics demanded that separate schools be guaranteed in the legislation which created the provinces. Since Laurier felt that he could not force on the country his desire to protect the French-Canadian and Catholic minorities in these provinces, it was necessary to remove this guarantee from the proposed legislation and to leave the matter for men of goodwill to solve in time to come.

Laurier explained his position in a letter to the Editor of the Montreal newspaper, *The Witness,* which was a militant champion of Protestantism :

> Dear Mr. Dougall :
>
> [The "Witness" has always been so generous to me that you must not be surprised if I attach to its criticism a greater weight than to that of any other paper.
>
> Will you permit me therefore to place before you the views which have influenced me in the education clauses of the bills

for the admission of the new Provinces of Alberta and Saskatchewan into the Dominion ?

I need not remind you that upon many questions, Confederation was a compromise. It is doubtful if Confederation could have been established without important sacrifices of opinion on many points.

The education clause of the B.N.A. Act was the most remarkable of all and in that clause George Brown, who was a most determined opponent of separate schools, agreed not only to admit the system in his own province, but to make its continuance part of the Constitution. Nor is this all, but a similar provision was made for the minority of any province which might enter the Dominion with a system of separate schools.] Can you doubt that if the provinces of Alberta and Saskatchewan had been admitted into the Dominion in 1867 instead of 1905, they would have received the same treatment as was given to Ontario and Quebec ? I do not think that this can be denied.

The Proposition in the bill is to give the minority the guarantee of the continuance of their system of schools as they would have had it in 1867.

[I am well aware that the idea of having schools partaking of ecclesiastical domination is repugnant to the spirit of our age. Even such an objection could not hold against the spirit of the constitution, but I truly believe the true character of the schools in the Northwest Territories is not known; under the name of separate schools they are really national.

The law of the Northwest Territories subjects separate schools to the following conditions :

1. All teachers must hold their diplomas from the Board of Public Instruction.

2. All schools must be examined and controlled by Inspectors appointed by the Board of Public Instruction.

3. All books used therein must be the books approved by the Board of Public Instruction.

4. The tuition of the pupils must be in the English language. This secular instruction is absolutely under the control of the provincial authorities. The only privilege in religious matters is that at 3:30 p.m., such religious instruction can be given to the pupils as is thought advisable by the trustees of the schools.

Do you not believe that children so instructed can make good Canadians ?] Why, then, refuse to do for this minority what has been done for the minority of Quebec and the minority of Ontario ? If this be refused, the minority of the Northwest Territories will smart under a sense of wrong and injustice. [They will believe that the public faith of the country is violated against them and to their prejudice, and who will pronounce their complaint unfounded ?]

> For my part, I feel very strongly that it is essential — as essential now as it was in 1867 — to make all parties feel sure that under our British constitution, in our Confederation, the first duty is to keep faith, with all classes in the very manner which was set down as the basis of our Dominion. [If this is not the idea that ought to guide us in this matter, I confess that I made an error, but if it is, you will agree with me that I am following the right course.]
>
> Believe me, as ever, dear Mr. Dougall,
>
> > Yours very sincerely,
> > Wilfrid Laurier.

French Canadians are still waiting for the goodwill, sympathy and understanding of men in order to realize the dream of Laurier.

The settlement of the West was not possible, of course, without some attention being given to the development of Canada's trans-continental system of railways. The railway policy of the Liberal party is an interesting one, and its record is also interesting. In 1897, the Canadian Government arrived at an agreement with the Canadian Pacific Railway concerning the extension of the line towards the Crow's Nest Pass. The Government agreed to help financially with the building of this line on the condition that the CPR would grant a substantial reduction in the shipping rates between central Canada and the western provinces. Secondly, the Government extended the Inter-Colonial Railway of the Maritimes to Montreal. Then in 1903 came the Government's announcement that the time had arrived for the building of new trans-continental lines, to supplement the Canadian Pacific Railway, in order to provide another exit for the products of the West to the Ocean, and this at the least possible cost.

The new trans-continental lines would also permit the shipment of industrial Eastern goods to the West, again at the cheapest possible cost. At least, these are the reasons the Government gave at the time. It has since been suggested that the Liberals wanted to build a trans-continental railway because the Conservatives before them had built one. It has also been suggested that Laurier didn't really understand such practical matters as the construction of railways. It used to be said :

The only figures he ever understood were figures of speech.

In the following speech, in which he presented the Government's railway policy, Laurier spoke — eloquently as always — as if the idea of a transcontinental railway had never been thought of before :

[First, Sir, perhaps it would not be amiss if I were to address myself at once to a question which has come to us from different quarters, and which may find an echo within these walls. Why this new enterprise ? Why this expenditure ? Why should Parliament be called upon to assent to such a policy as is here indicated ?] We ask Parliament to assent to this policy because we believe — nay, we feel certain, and certain beyond a doubt — that in so doing we give voice and expression to a sentiment, which is today in the mind, and still more in the heart, of every Canadian, that a railway to extend from the shores of the Atlantic Ocean to the shores of the Pacific Ocean, and to be, every inch of it, on Canadian soil, is a national as well as a commercial necessity. That such a road must be built, [that it is, in the language which I have used, a national and a commercial necessity,] that it is a corollary of our status as a nation, that it is a requisite of our commercial development, is a proposition to which up to this moment, I have heard no dissent.

[Exception has been taken to the immediate necessity of building such a road, exception has been taken to the policy which we have to suggest for the immediate construction of such a road; but as to the idea itself I have never heard a word of opposition, nor do I believe that such a word will be heard in the debate. The first of these objections, that is to the immediate construction of such a road, can be disposed of, I believe, with a single observation.] To those who urge upon us the policy of tomorrow, and tomorrow, and tomorrow; to those who tell us, Wait, wait, wait; to those who advise us to pause, to consider, to reflect, to calculate and to inquire, our answer is : [No, this is not a time for deliberation,] this is a time for action. The flood tide is upon us that leads on to fortune; if we let it pass it may never recur again. If we let it pass, the voyage of our national life, bright as it is today, will be bound in shallows. We cannot wait, because time does not wait; we cannot wait because, in these days of wonderful development, time lost is doubly lost; we cannot wait, because at this moment there is a transformation going on in the conditions of our national life which it would be folly to ignore and a crime to overlook; we cannot wait, because the prairies of the North-West, which for countless ages have been roamed over by the wild herds of the bison, or by the scarcely less wild tribes of red men, are now invaded from all sides by the white race. They came last year one hundred thousand and still they come in still greater numbers.

The Government built its new railway both by extending exist-ing railways, such as the Grand Trunk and the Canadian Northern, in co-operation with the owners, and by adding its own lines.

The details of these transactions — highly profitable ones for a handful of speculators involved — are too complicated to go into here. But the result was that by 1914 Canada had over thirty thousand miles of railway — twelve thousand more than when Laurier had begun his project. And it had added not one, but two trans-continental lines to the Canadian Pacific project completed in the era of Sir John A. Macdonald. The new transcontinental lines created during the Laurier regime were to become, in time, the mainlines of the gigantic Canadian National Railways system.

Most of the bill — a gigantic one considering Canada's popu-lation at the time, was footed by the Government. Its own line — the "National Transcontinental", along with the Que-bec Bridge across the St. Lawrence, had cost one hundred and fifty-five million dollars. In addition the Government guaranteed thirty-five million dollars of the Grand Trunk Pacific Company's bonds, and several more millions of the Canadian Northern Company's. The historian Arthur Lower has described the Liberals' railway project as "the most gorgeous spending spree in Canadian peace-time history".

If, like Macdonald before him, Laurier built a transcontinental rail system to help tie the provinces together physically, un-like Macdonald he also made attempts to tie them together in other ways. From the beginning — even when Confederation was in the planning stages — Macdonald had come out strongly in favour of a strong central government, and after Confederation he had acted accordingly, sometimes antagoniz-ing the provinces in the process. Laurier, on the other hand, sought to ease regional difficulties. He surrounded himself with men who were essentially "provincial rights" men, and he made almost no use of the federal government's power to "disallow" provincial legislation.

Laurier's government insisted on closer cooperation between the federal and provincial governments as a means of solving common problems. [Whereas Macdonald had refused to attend the first inter-provincial conference of 1887, seeing it as a revolt of the provinces, Laurier gave his blessing to similar conferences in 1902 and 1906. Significantly these conferences produced no great criticisms of the federal government.]

There is no doubt that the economic boom which occurred during Laurier's regime helped to create this atmosphere of tolerance and co-operation within Canada. It also helped Canada's relations with foreign powers, especially the United States. Even reciprocity with the U.S., which had been given up as a lost cause at the beginning of Laurier's regime, became a definite possibility by 1910. On February 27 of that year the British ambassador to Washington intimated to the American government that the British government would like the United States to undertake any proposed negotiations directly with Ottawa. Only a week later an American delegation was in Ottawa discussing a trade proposal with the Canadian government. On May 20, 1910, a Toronto newspaper printed a message from President Taft, assuring the Canadian people that :

> It is my deliberate purpose to promote in such ways as are open to me better trade relations between the United States and Canada than at present exist. I am profoundly convinced that these two countries, touching each other for more than three thousand miles, have common interests in trade and require special arrangements in legislation and administration which are not involved in the relations of the United States with countries beyond the Seas.

Formal negotiations for reciprocity between Canada and the United States opened in Ottawa on November 4, 1910. Almost three months later details of the agreement were published. The agreement provided that the proposals would be submitted to Congress and to Parliament, and that they would come into effect in either country at the moment they became law in the other.

However, long though the fight had been to obtain a reciprocal trade agreement with the United States, the announcement that it was almost a reality met with a great deal of opposition. The leader of the Conservative party, Robert Borden, stated the policy of his party in the House of Commons:

> The Conservative Party stands to-day as it stood in the past, for the policy of reciprocity within the British Empire. As far as we are concerned we believe that the aim of the fiscal legislation of this country ought to be to promote that great end and purpose, and we believe that for that purpose, as well as for the purpose of fiscal freedom in every possible respect we ought to keep ourselves free of all entangling treaties or alliances or understandings, that that object and purpose which I regard as the greatest consideration that could be before the eyes of any Canadian statesman today, should be kept before our minds and that everything that would lessen the possibility, probability and imminence of carrying out that great scheme of reciprocity within the Empire ought to be banished from our minds and put aside as unworthy of our attention.

Opposition also came from the business community of Canada. One of the most outspoken individuals opposing the reciprocity agreement was Sir Clifford Sifton, former minister in Laurier's government, who insisted that Canada was putting its head into a noose. Sifton once stated his opposition in the following words :

> For the last thirty or forty years we have been either ignored or buffeted by the United States and during that time we have taken our way, we have proceeded serenely, under the strong protective arm of the British Empire. Up to this present time we have been somewhat of a nuisance to the Empire; but now when we come to a point where we may be of use to the Empire, [when we can send men and ships, if necessary, to her aid, then when we can be of some use to the Empire that gave us our liberty and our traditions of citizenship —] at the first beckoning hand from Washington we turn to listen; the first time anyone beckons we turn from the path that leads to the centre of the Empire and take the path that leads to Washington. So far as I am concerned, I say 'Not for me' and finally, I ask, Is it safe for 7½ millions to bargain with 90 millions ? We may say we will take their terms but not pay the price. Sir, I think such a course is neither sane nor wise. If we take the terms we will have to pay the price.

The subject of reciprocity was also debated hotly in the United States, of course, and some of the statements that emanated from there gave the Canadian opponents grist for their mill in the fight against the treaty. One congressman, for example, said :

106

I am for it because I hope to see the day when the American flag will float over every square foot of the British North American possessions, clear to the North Pole. They speak our language, their institutions are much like ours, they are trained in the difficult art of self-government. My judgement is that if the Treaty of 1854 had never been abrogated the chances of a consolidation of the two countries would have been much greater than they are now. I have no doubt whatever that the day is not far distant when Great Britain will joyfully see all her North American possessions become part of this Republic. That is the way things are tending now.

Even though President Taft insisted that the agreement had no political significance, many Canadians were not convinced. After all, in February 1911, a senator had presented a resolution requesting the president :

... to enter upon and prosecute from time to time such negotiations with the British government as he may deem expedient for the annexation of the Dominion of Canada to the United States of America.

A Democrat from New York put forward the same idea a little more subtly :

This reciprocity pact is the greatest economic advantage of the age. We have almost obliterated the frontier line and a few years of commercial peace will do the rest.

However, in Canada it was to be the public, not the politicians, who would decide the fate of the proposed reciprocity agreement. For the federal elections were due, and the question of Canada-U.S. trade was to be one of the two main issues. The other was a proposed bill to create a Canadian Navy. This proposal was fought by the more extreme French-Canadian nationalists, under Henri Bourassa. Bourassa argued that the creation of a Canadian navy meant automatic participation by Canada in Imperial wars which were no concern of French Canadians. In order to fight Laurier on his imperial policy Bourassa joined forces with Robert Borden, leader of the Conservatives. It was an unnatural alliance, for the two had nothing else in common.

But the main issue in the election of 1911 was the reciprocity proposal, and it was debated across the country by politicians, journalists, businessmen, pamphleteers, and even the clergy.

A spirit of nationalism, a feeling that Canada could "go it alone", fear that reciprocity *would* mean annexation to the United States, fear of endangering relations with the mother country, and the pleasure that came from telling a bigger brother where to get off — all of these explain why, on September 21, 1911, Laurier's Liberal government was defeated. The destinies of the nation fell once more into the hands of the Conservatives. Where the new government would lead the Canadian nation, no one really knew in 1911. However, there was no doubt that it would have to continue to support the dynamic Canadian nationalism which had been created during the Laurier era.

Robert L. Borden, the new prime minister, inherited a house in good order. Laurier had served his people well. Borden had a good example to follow.

# CANADA TO THE WOLVES (I)      10
## The Washington Conference of 1871

No study of Canadian history from 1867 would be complete without some detailed examination of Canada's growth as an autonomous power.

In 1867, when the main British colonies in North America united to form the Dominion of Canada, the new nation had no treaty-making power. All of her external affairs were managed by the Crown. The Queen's representative, the Governor-General of Canada, was the official channel through which directives in external relations and Imperial matters were given to the Canadian government. And it was through the Governor-General that the Canadian government communicated with the Imperial government.

It was not until after the First World War that Canada assumed responsibility for her own relations with other countries, but she had been well prepared for this by two of Canada's great prime ministers, John A. Macdonald and Wilfrid Laurier.

Although they led opposing parties in the Canadian parliament, Macdonald and Laurier shared a common desire : namely to advance Canada's position in international affairs *as a member of the British Empire*. Different though their thinking may have been on many internal matters, both Macdonald and Laurier wanted to maintain Canada's connection with Great Britain.

To Macdonald, the first prime minister, one of the main reasons for maintaining the British connection was to make it possible for the new Dominion to grow to true nationhood. Without the strength and might of Great Britain behind her, he feared, Canada might easily be absorbed into the United States. Relations between Britain and the United States were far from friendly in the period following the American Civil War, in which Britain had openly taken the Confederate side. Threats of war were common, and they were frequently accompanied by demands for the annexation of Canada to the United States. Macdonald once expressed his view on the imperial connection as follows :

> I am satisfied that the vast majority of the people of Canada are in favour of the continuance and perpetuation of the connection between the Dominion and the mother country. There is nothing to gain and everything to lose by separation. I believe that if any party or person were to announce or declare such a thing, whether by annexation with the neighbouring country — the great republic to the south of us, or by declaring independence, I believe that the people of Canada would say "No". We are content, we are prosperous, we have prospered under the flag of England; and I say that it would be unwise, that we should be lunatics, to change the certain present happiness for the uncertain chances of the future. I always remember, when this occurs to me, the Italian epitaph : "I was well, I would be better, and here I am." We are well, as we know, all are well, and I am satisfied that the majority of the people of Canada are of the same opinion which I now venture to express here.

But, to Macdonald, being content to live under the flag of Great Britain did not mean being content to give up Canada's right to a voice in her own affairs.

For example, Macdonald had himself been present at the founding, in 1884 in England, of the Imperial Federation

League, the main aim of which was to increase the strength of the Empire — economically in the face of a continuing depression of trade, and militarily in the face of a rising Germany.

However, although Macdonald was a supporter of the Imperial Federation League, he made it clear that there were certain interpretations of the term "imperial federation" which he could not accept. Here are his comments on the subject :

> It depends upon what you mean by Imperial federation. The proposal that there should be a parliamentary federation of the Empire I regard as impracticable. I greatly doubt whether England would agree that the Parliament which has sat during so many centuries at Westminster should be made subsidiary to a federal legislature.
>
> But however that might be, I am quite sure that Canada would never consent to be taxed by a central body sitting in London, in which she would have practically no voice; for her proportionate number of members in such an assembly would amount to little more than an honorary representation. That form of imperial federation is an idle dream. So, alas, in my judgment, is the proposal to establish a uniform tariff throughout the Empire. No colony would ever surrender its right to control its fiscal policy.

Macdonald was obviously not willing to let Canada lose its voice in any matter which concerned it. He was given a chance to prove that he meant what he said when he served as a member of the British delegation to the Washington Conference in 1871. His activities there, as the only Canadian representative, are the subject of this program. In it we shall attempt to show how far Macdonald was willing to go in protecting Canada's autonomy, even when it meant antagonizing Her Majesty's representatives.

Here is the background to the historic Washington conference :

Its main purpose was to settle some of the disagreements between Britain and the United States left over from the American Civil War in which, as we have said, Britain had sided openly with the Confederates. Canada's main aim, however, was to settle a dispute with the United States over fishing rights. Between 1854 and 1864, when a reciprocity treaty existed between the States and Canada, there was no such dispute, but when, at the end of the Civil War, the Americans abrogated the treaty, earlier rules — established in 1818, came back into force. Under them, American vessels were permitted to use Canadian ports for shelter, to make repairs, and to take on wood and water. But the American fishermen, accustomed during the reciprocity period to fishing in the Canadian coastal waters, continued to exercise this former privilege. The Canadians imposed a license fee, but some of the Americans refused to pay it. In January of 1870, Macdonald decided to act. He fitted out six cruisers, and some American fishing boats were seized. The Americans complained, and it was even stated by the *New York Times* that :

> ... the fisheries problem is such a one that only bloodshed can solve it.

The matter of fishing rights was put down on the agenda for the Washington Conference of 1871, and on the first of February of that year the Governor-General informed Sir John A. Macdonald that the British government wanted him to serve as one of the plenipotentiaries on the British high commission to the conference.

Macdonald's comments on the invitation are significant, for they indicate his awareness of the need for a Canadian voice in matters which concerned Canada :

> I have thought over Lord Kimberley's proposition that I shall act on the Joint Commission with the United States on fisheries and other matters. My first impression was that it would be better for Canada not to be represented on such a commission. But then we must consider that, if Canada allowed the matter to go by default, and left its interest to be adjudicated upon and settled by a commission composed exclusively of Americans having an adverse interest, and Englishmen having little or no interest in Canada, the government here would be very much censured if the results were a sacrifice of the rights of the Dominion. England would at once say that the offer to be represented on the Commission was made to Canada and that it was declined. Surrounded with difficulties as the matter seems to be, I think that, perhaps, the best answer to be given is this : that I will act on getting the consent of my colleagues.

After consultation with his colleagues, Macdonald accepted the invitation to form part of the Commission. Shortly before he left for Washington, he wrote to his old friend, Sir John Rose :

> I contemplate my visit to Washington with a good deal of anxiety, for if anything goes wrong I shall be like a scapegoat... at all events so far as Canada is concerned. However, I thought that after all Canada has done for me I should not shirk the responsibility.

The British delegation to the Washington Conference consisted of five representatives, including Macdonald, and it was headed by the Earl de Grey. In his capacity as plenipotentiary, Macdonald was a representative of Her Majesty's government. However, he was also the representative of Canada, which had different interests from those of Great Britain. Macdonald was to ride two horses. He left Ottawa for Washington on the 27th of February, accompanied by Lady Macdonald, and he described his first activities as follows :

> We found Sir Edward Thornton's carriage and one of his attachés, the Honourable Mr. Trench, awaiting us at the station. We have comfortable quarters at the Arlington, but the Commissioners have established a Bachelors' hall of their own, which will be gay enough as Lord de Grey is known to be hospitable, and has brought his cook with him. In company with Sir Edward, on Wednesday, I called upon Mr. Fish, with whom I had a short conversation, and consequently visited the American Commissioners, viz. General Schenck, Judge Nelson of the Supreme Court, Judge Hoar of Massachusetts, and Senator Williams... I subsequently went with Thornton to Mrs. Fish's reception, where I met and was introduced to a number of other swells... Of course I saw Lord de Grey and the other English commissioners during the day. Thus ends Wednesday's record.

The fisheries dispute was not the only matter on the agenda of the Washington conference, but as far as Macdonald was concerned it was the most important one. *To the English delegation, however, the Canadian fisheries were important only insofar as they were something they could give cheaply to the Americans in order to improve their relations with them.* This must be kept in mind in order to understand the actions of the English delegates at the Washington Conference. The chairman of the English group, the Earl de Grey, hoped that the Canadians would simply let the United States buy the right to fish within Canadian territorial waters — and this in perpetuity. Macdonald did not hesitate to correct his colleagues. Here is how he reported his argument with them, in a letter home :

> (I told them) that it would be out of the question for Canada to surrender, for all time to come, her fishery rights for any compensation however great — that we had no right to injure posterity by depriving Canada, either as a dependency or a nation, of her fisheries, and that in my opinion any surrender must be for an unspecified period but liable to be terminated by either party.
>
> [(I told them) that the fisheries are valuable in themselves, and would, with increasing population, become annually more valuable.]
>
> But the value of the catch is of less consequence than the means which the exclusive enjoyment of the fisheries gave us of improving our position as a maritime power. (I told them) that Canada possesses infinitely more valuable fisheries than the United States, with better harbours, and that if we pursued the exclusive system vigorously we might run a winning race with the U.S. as a maritime power ...

After hearing Macdonald's arguments, the Earl de Grey proposed to the Americans that the fisheries be exchanged for some reciprocal trade arrangements. But the Americans rejected the plan, and the British government authorized de Grey to discuss the sale of the fisheries — in spite of the fact that Macdonald insisted they were Canada's property and could not be sold without her consent. Finally, it was suggested that a clause be inserted in the treaty to the effect that its provisions would be subject to ratification by the Canadian parliament. Macdonald was in quandary, as he explained to his chief lieutenant in the government, Sir Charles Tupper, in a letter dated March 21 :

> This instruction places me in a exceedingly embarrassing position. If a majority of my colleagues should at any time conclude to accept terms which I do not approve of, I must, of course, either protest and withdraw, or remain on the Commission and trust to the non-ratification of the treaty by Canada.
>
> If I take the first course it will disclose to the Americans the existence of a difference of opinion — a conflict, in fact — between Canada and England. This the Americans are anxious to establish, in order to get up a sort of quarrel between the two, and to strengthen the party in England which desires to get rid of the colonies as a burden.
>
> If I continue to act on the Commission I shall be attacked for making an unworthy sacrifice of Canada's rights, and may be compelled to vote in Parliament against a treaty which I had a share in making. I must manage matters, however, as best I can, according to the circumstances ...

The following day Macdonald sent a telegram to Tupper, reporting on the latest developments :

> Monday we resumed fishery question and repeated our desire to obtain reciprocity treaty in principle as an equivalent. Americans stated that was impossible, but offered one million dollars for the fisheries in perpetuity. We made the offer to take free : fish, salt, coal, lumber and coasting trade. They refused the coasting trade at once. We then offered to leave out the coasting trade and take instead a sum of money to be settled hereafter. After long consideration they offered free coal and salt, and free admission into their market of mackerel, herring and cod. Also to allow lumber free from first July 1876. And they desired mutual free fishing in the lakes and the St. Lawrence above St. Regis, but not in the streams falling into them. They admit that coal and salt must be free in December next. We think they may be induced to consent to make all fish free, and perhaps to free lumber at an earlier date. They refuse any additional money payment. All this was to be for a term of years to be agreed upon, and on two years notice afterwards. I do not think it likely they will offer better terms. Please send me decision of council.

The answer of the Canadian Cabinet came quickly :

> Council considers terms offered in your telegram of the 22nd as so inadequate to the value of the fisheries in Canada that no government could carry a proposal so obnoxious to the people through our parliament. Although very anxious to settle this question, such a solution would only make matters worse, as great irritation must follow the certain rejection, by the Parliament of Canada, of the terms proposed.

So Macdonald had to reject the Americans' offer. Macdonald's fellow commissioners were becoming impatient with his insistence that Canada have her way. One of them described the Canadian prime minister as :

> ... a pain in the neck and a colonial obstructing the march of the Empire.

However, although Macdonald intended to deal firmly with the English commissioners, at the same time he did not want himself or Canada to be held responsible for a breach of negotiations between the United States and Great Britain, and, as he put it :

> ... thus strengthen the hands of the party in England who consider Canada a burden to be got on without, and an obstacle to friendly relations with the United States.

Macdonald was going to have to make a compromise in the long run, but there was still more fighting to be done. On April 15, after six weeks of deadlock the Americans made another proposal. They offered to buy the Canadian fisheries for a number of years at a price to be settled by arbitration. They even suggested that they might be prepared to accept the duty-free entry of fish.

Macdonald's counter proposal was that the Americans pay, in addition, one hundred and fifty thousand dollars a year, plus another fifty thousand dollars a year until their duty on Canadian lumber had been removed. When Lord de Grey, chairman of the British delegation, protested that Macdonald was asking too much, Macdonald told him :

> ... that I was satisfied that the present proposition would not be acceptable to Canada in any sense — that the fisheries were our property, that we should be the judge of what their value was to us, and that we would fix our price, and if the buyer would not pay the price, then we would keep our property.

Finally, in desperation, the British government resorted to a kind of bribery to swing Macdonald around to their side. One of the matters which Canada had hoped to discuss at the Washington Conference was that of compensation for damage done by Fenian invaders from the United States into Canada between 1866 and 1871. The Fenians were Irish nationalists who invaded Canada at many points along the border as a means of wreaking revenge on their traditional enemy, the English. As the Fenians had entered Canada by way of the United States, the Canadian government wanted to hold the American government responsible for the considerable damage and the loss of lives they had caused. The American government preferred to remain neutral in the matter because in many parts of the United States the Irish vote was important.

Lord de Grey, by now convinced that Macdonald could not be made to change his mind on the fisheries question by mere persuasion, told the prime minister that he was prepared to ask the British government to pay Canada a sum of money to get rid of the Fenian question. After consultation with the

British government, de Grey was authorized to convey to Macdonald, in the strictest confidence, the decision of Her Majesty's government : It would, he reported, agree to compensate Canada for the damages caused by the Fenians *if other matters were settled*.

By "other matters" the British government meant, of course, the matter of the fisheries. Then, after tempting Sir John with money to make him more co-operative, Earl de Grey proceeded to hint rather strongly that if he did not co-operate with the English delegates, Macdonald would be injuring his own country. [He pointed out that the English delegates — even Sir Stafford Northcote, who was in the opposition party in the British government — thought as one man on the subjects under discussion at the Washington Conference.] He warned Macdonald that if he did not vote *with* them :

> ...Canada will have no friends in the British Parliament.

These were powerful incentives and powerful arguments, and Macdonald was fully aware of the serious consequences which might result from too much stubbornness on his part. At the same time he was convinced of the rightness of his own position.

He suggested to Lord de Grey that it might be best for him either to absent himself from the conference, or to attend and state that he did not believe the American proposal would be accepted by the Canadian parliament. The British commissioners were taken aback by Macdonald's attitude, and decided to postpone everything until further instructions had been received from England. When they came, they were to the effect that the British delegation was to accept the last proposal of the American government — that is, the offer to purchase the Canadian fisheries for a specified number of years — that number, and the price, to be settled later by arbitration. Macdonald considered resigning his commission as plenipotentiary of the British government, but he had second thoughts:

> After thinking it over for a night, however, I refrained from doing so, reserving to myself the right of ulterior action.

The "ulterior action" Macdonald had in mind was refusing to sign the treaty, but he had second thoughts on that too, as he explained in a letter to Sir John Rose :

> I at first thought of declining to sign the treaty. That would have been the easiest and most popular course for me to pursue *quo ad* Canada and my position there, (and *entre-nous,* my colleagues at Ottawa pressed me to do.) But my declining to sign might have involved such terrible consequences that I finally made up my mind to make the sacrifice of my popularity and position in Canada... Had I refused to sign, it would have been accepted as conclusive evidence that Canada would reject the proposition. The treaty would therefore have gone to the Senate with the fishery question left, in fact, an open one, and this would have ensured its rejection by that body. If the treaty were lost in the Senate, matters would be worse than ever. The hopeful expection of the people of the United States would be changed to a feeling of great irritation; and, in fact, the conviction would force itself upon everybody's mind that there was no chance of a peaceable solution of the difficulties between the two countries, and the only solution would be war, whenever the United States thought they might profitably undertake it.

On May 8, 1871, at ten o'clock in the morning Macdonald and the other High Commissioners and the American delegates appeared at the State Department for the final ceremony of the conference. Donald Creighton, in his biography of Sir John A. Macdonald*, describes the scene as follows :

> The room was sweet with bright masses of spring flowers, and on the sideboard an unusual but not unappetising morning collation. Strawberries and ice-cream lay waiting to be eaten. A relaxed feeling of accomplishment was in the air. Macdonald alone did not share it. He was only too well aware that something that he did not want, but could not prevent, was about to be done, and done irrevocably. [Even as they chatted a little nervously together, and exchanged photographs and autographs the seals were being affixed to the two precious copies of the treaty by an awkward and extremely nervous clerk, whose operations were not assisted when Tenderden, that most invaluable of secretaries, dropped quantities of burning sealing wax on his fingers. The poor man somewhat inauspiciously burst into tears when the work was done. But done it was, and the copies lay ready on the table.] Then the final, solemn act began. Macdonald being the junior member of the British commission, was one of the last to sign. In a half whisper he said to Fish of the American delegation :

* Donald Creighton : *John A. Macdonald : The Old Chieftain,* p. 102. Excerpt reproduced by permission of The Macmillan Company of Canada.

THE APPRENTICESHIP

"Well, here go the fisheries."

Fish countered swiftly :

"You get a good equivalent for them."

"No — we give them away. Here goes the signature !"

Macdonald signed his name with the usual small flourish under the final "D", and rose from the table, saying :

"They are gone."

---

Macdonald's return to Canada was hardly a triumphant one. The Liberals, and many others whom the Toronto *Globe* and other newspapers had incited, greeted him with a storm of denunciation, seeing in him a man who had sacrificed Canada. He was compared to Judas Iscariot and Benedict Arnold rolled into one. Macdonald put up with the criticism and the outbursts of nationalism. His moment came on May 3, 1872, a year following the conclusion of the Washington Conference, when he addressed the Canadian Parliament :

> How eagerly I was watched during these twelve months ! If the government should come out in favour of the treaty then it was to be taken as a betrayal of the people of Canada. If the government should come out against the treaty, then the First Minister was to be charged with opposing the interests of the Empire. Whichever course we might take they were lying in wait with some mode of attack. But "silence is golden", Mr. Speaker, and I kept silent. I believe the sober second thought of this country accords with the sober second thought of the Government, and we come down here and ask the people of Canada, through their representatives, to accept this treaty, to accept it with all its imperfections, to accept it for the sake of peace, and for the sake of the great Empire of which we form a part.

The Treaty of Washington was duly ratified by Canada, and was brought into force by proclamation on July 1, 1873. It may have failed to restore the provisions of the Treaty of 1854, for reciprocal free trade, but it nevertheless kept the peace, and for twelve years there was tranquility along Canadian shores.

However, a more important result of the Washington Conference was the change it brought in the way Canada and

England looked upon each other. The Canadians were convinced that the mother country was willing to sacrifice Canada's interests for her own good if need be. And the English realized that Canada had come to think of herself as a nation with a right to a voice in its own affairs. Even though England finally succeeded in telling Canada what to do at the Washington Conference, she could never again take it for granted that Canada would *always* be ready to obey.

# CANADA TO THE WOLVES (II)    11
## The Aftermath of the
## Washington Conference of 1871

Sir John A. Macdonald's first foray into international imperial relations had proved disastrous as far as he was concerned. He returned from the Washington Conference of 1871 pessimistic over the future membership of Canada in the Empire. He felt that in time Canadians would secede from the British Empire since the British government appeared to have no real interest in protecting the colonies as they grew internationally, and since Britain seemed prepared to immolate Canada on the altar of Anglo-American friendship. He also felt that British statesmen were contemptuous of Canadian colonial interests and he feared very much that English liberalism might very well demand that the colonies declare themselves independent and leave the bosom of the mother country. Macdonald once wrote to his old friend Lord Carnarvon, the British colonial secretary :

> We are glad to know that we have in you a friend. I may almost say a friend in need, for we greatly distrust the men at the helm in England, who cannot, I feel, be considered as appreciating the importance of maintaining the Empire as it is, intact... We may perhaps be obliged to appeal from the government to the people of England!

It was therefore evident to Canadian nationalists that if Canada could not rely on British diplomats to present Canada's needs on the international scene effectively and with sympathy, it would be necessary for Canada to devise some method whereby these needs would be made known and respected. Between 1871 and the first quarter of the twentieth century not a single year went by without Canada insisting to Great Britain that she be given a voice in international affairs when discussions centered on matters which affected her.

Macdonald had signed the Treaty of Washington in 1871 as a British plenipotentiary, and not as a Canadian representative. He had been bitterly disillusioned at the constant willingness of his English colleagues to veto him whenever the interests of Canada conflicted with those of Britain in her relationships with the United States. However, this precedent was followed in 1874 when George Brown went to Washington, first as a confidential agent, and then — on the insistence of the Canadian government, as a British plenipotentiary to discuss a reciprocity treaty with the United States.

Three years later, in the arbitration of the Halifax fisheries dispute, Alexander Tilloch Galt, one of the founding fathers of the country, was present as a British commissioner. The Canadian government was represented by a Canadian counsel, but Galt, too, presented the Canadian case. Galt was a Canadian nationalist at heart, and when there was a conflict between Imperial patriotism and Canadian nationalism he always decided in favour of the latter.

Like Macdonald, Galt did not expect much from British diplomats. When he was appointed to the British commission to arbitrage the Halifax fisheries dispute in 1877, Galt wrote to Macdonald, expressing his fear that he would not receive, as he put it :

...proper support from the Imperial government who invariably show undue anxiety to conciliate the Yankees. A common danger threatens the British and Spanish possessions in America through the preponderance of the United States. The danger is not one of violence, as the people of the United States are not favourable to such a cause. It consists in the establishment of such a state of commercial dependence upon them as will centre there all the national interests of the adjoining countries and then gradually draw them into the union. In the case of Canada this policy is openly avowed; in that of Cuba it is equally active.

The experiences of the Washington Treaty of 1871, of the trade discussions of 1874, and of the Halifax fisheries dispute in 1877 demonstrated to the Canadian government the necessity of establishing an effective liaison with the British government. The normal channel of communication between the two governments was the Governor-General, but his effectiveness was decreased considerably by the fact that in many respects he was an imperial agent, and by the fact that correspondence took a long time to cross the ocean.

The Canadian government decided that the time had come to appoint a Canadian agent in London, to serve as her official representative. The Canadians wanted him to have diplomatic status in order to express the Canadian government's point of view in all international and imperial matters with which Canada was concerned. Furthermore the Canadian representative was to be empowered to negotiate commercial treaties and agreements in association with the British representative. This arrangement would be something unparalleled in British colonial history. But the Canadians did not feel that it was asking too much. As Alexander Tilloch Galt pointed out :

Canada has ceased to occupy the position of an ordinary possession of the Crown. She exists in the form of a powerful central government, having already no less than seven subordinate local executive and legislative systems, soon to be largely augmented by the development of the vast regions lying between Lake Superior and the Rocky Mountains.

Prime Minister Macdonald agreed with this, for he wrote in the margin of Galt's memorandum :

The sooner the Dominion is treated as an auxiliary power rather than as a dependency, the sooner we will assume all responsibilities of the position, including the settlement of its contribution to the defence of the Empire whenever and wherever assailed.

However, Macdonald had second thoughts and never sent this addition he had made to Galt's memorandum.

Canada's desire for diplomatic status for her representative in London was not well received by the British government, which felt that the position of the Canadian representative :

> ... would necessarily be more analogous to that of an officer in the Home service than to that of a minister at a foreign court.

Macdonald had no interest in getting involved in an argument over the matter with the British government. He felt that in time the Canadian representative in London — whatever his status — would be able to establish his position firmly.

There ensued a bit of a scuffle between the two governments over the representative's title. Macdonald had hoped to call him "resident minister". The British authorities preferred "Canadian Representative" or "Dominion Representative" or "Canadian Commissioner." The Canadians came back with "High Commissioner of Canada in London." The British government countered with another suggestion : "Special Commissioner." This one Macdonald rejected outright, explaining rather bluntly to the British authorities that the Canadian envoy would not be going to England for any special purpose, but to represent Canada's interests generally. Macdonald wrote :

> It seems to me that it is a matter of no importance to the Imperial Parliament what title we may give our agent. We might call him *nuncio* or *legate a latere gurnatoris* if we please. It is of course for the imperial government to settle the status of our agent in England under whatever title he may present himself. Since the title of Resident Minister is objected to, I think we must adhere to that of High Commissioner.

And there the matter ended. The appointment of the High Commissioner to London was of immense importance not only with respect to Canada's relations with England and the Empire, but also with respect to her relations with the United States. When the Canadian government had been urging the appointment of a representative in London, its memorandum had stated categorically that Canada was to be :

... even more responsible than the Imperial government for the maintenance of international relations towards the United States, a subject which will yearly require greater prudence and care, as the population of the two countries extend along, and mingle across, the vast frontier line 3,000 miles in length.

The first high commissioner appointed to London was Alexander Tilloch Galt, who held the post from 1880 to 1883. Although he became quite dissatisfied with his position, especially over the vagueness of his diplomatic status and over lack of money to establish the social position which he felt he should have, he did succeed in having the British Government pay attention to the Canadian view. Galt was succeeded by Sir Charles Tupper, who remained in the position until 1896, when he was recalled to lead the Conservative party in the federal election of that year.

Just how independent Canada had become in its thinking — and in its actions — by this time is indicated in a letter Prime Minister Macdonald sent to his High Commissioner in London in 1885. The subject was a proposal — from Britain — that Canada send an official force to take part in the Sudan expedition. Macdonald wrote to Tupper :

> We do not stand at all in the same position as Autralasia. The Suez Canal is nothing to us, and we do not ask England to quarrel with France or Germany for our sakes... Why should we waste money and men in this wretched business ? England is not at war... Our men and money would therefore be sacrificed to get Gladstone and Co. out of the hole they have plunged themselves into by their own imbecility.

> Again, the reciprocal aid to be given by the Colonies and England should be a matter of treaty, deliberately entered into and settled on a permanent basis. The spasmodic offers of our Militia Colonels, anxious for excitement or notoriety, have roused unreasonable expectations in England, and are so far unfortunate. I dare say that a battalion or two of venturous spirits might be enlisted, but 7d. a day will cool most men's warlike ardour.

When Galt was High Commissioner in London he had been sent to Madrid and Paris with a British trade delegation, and although he had been consulted he had taken no part in the actual negotiations. When Tupper was High Commissioner he succeeded in achieving plenipotentiary status for himself in the negotiation of trade treaties between Canada and Spain and Canada and France — an important step. This was in 1892 and 1893. At the Colonial Conference of 1894 a resolution was adopted on this matter. It read :

> That provisions should be made by Imperial legislation enabling the dependencies of the Empire to enter into agreements of commercial reciprocity, including power of making differential tariffs, with Great Britain or with one another.
>
> (That) any provision in existing treaties between Great Britain and any foreign power which prevents the self-governing dependencies of the Empire from entering into agreements of commercial reciprocity with each other, or with Great Britain, should be removed.

Naturally the British authorities objected. On June 28, 1895, the Secretary of State for Colonies, Lord Ripon, sent a circular to Canada in which he expressed his extreme fear over the proposals made by the Colonial Conference :

> ...This policy involves a complete reversal of the fiscal and commercial system which was deliberately adopted by Great Britain half a century ago, and which has been maintained and extended ever since... While Parliament has removed all legislative restrictions in the colonies, so far as Imperial legislation is concerned, it will be necessary, in order that Her Majesty's government may be in a position to give effect to their responsibility for the international obligations of the Empire, and for the protection of its general interests, that any Bill passed by a colonial legislature providing for the imposition of differential duties should be reserved for the signification of Her Majesty's pleasure, so as to allow full opportunity for its consideration from these points of view.

This however, proved unacceptable to the Canadians, and they decided to follow her own course. In 1897 Canada adopted a tariff which violated the instructions of the colonial secretary. This action is now considered by some to be nothing short of a declaration of independence.

It is interesting to note that this new move towards independent action was engendered by a new phase in Canadian-American relations. It was in 1887 that the Secretary of State in Washington accepted the idea that Canada was a nation. When he was visited that year by Sir Charles Tupper, the secretary of State insisted that Canada was a nation, and said that, consequently, his country :

... may as well discuss public questions from that point of view.

It was to the advantage of the United States to recognize Canada as a nation. The American government had found that having to deal with the government of Canada through the government of Great Britain was cumbersome. In May, 1887 the Secretary of State referred to this unwieldy arrangement in a letter to Sir Charles Tupper :

> In the interview afforded by your visit I referred to the embarrassment arising out of the gradual practical emancipation of Canada from the control of the Mother Country and the consequent assumption by that community of attributes of autonomous and separate sovereignty, not, however, distinct from the Empire of Great Britain. The awkwardness of this imperfectly developed sovereignty is felt most strongly by the United States, which cannot have formal relations with Canada, except indirectly and as a colonial dependence of the British Crown, and nothing could better illustrate the embarrassment arising from this amorphous condition of things than the volumes of correspondence published severally this year relating to the fisheries by the United States, Great Britain, and the government of the Dominion. The time lost in this circumlocution, although often regrettable, was the least part of the difficulty, and the indirectness of appeal and reply was the most serious feature, ending, as it did, very unsatisfactorily.

The Secretary of State hoped that Sir Charles Tupper would be appointed British plenipotentiary in the forthcoming negotiations over the question of the fisheries. — Fisheries, fisheries, fisheries ! They seem to have been a constant source of difficulties between Canada and the United States. By the Washington Treaty of 1871 it had been agreed that the amount of compensation to be given Canada by the United States for ten years of fishing rights in Canadian coastal waters was to be determined by an arbitration board. In June, 1877, a majority of the commission members stipulated that a sum of $5,500,000, payable over a period of 12 years, would be an adequate price. The American representative dissented, however, and the agreement was badly received in his country. In 1886 the arrangement made at Halifax nine years earlier was cancelled, and the rules in force prior to the Washington Conference were once again applicable. In other words, Americans were not allowed to fish in Canadian coastal waters.

The Canadian government therefore began to warn off, detain, or seize United States vessels encroaching on Canadian waters. In 1886 alone, 49 American vessels were seized, and the Canadian government passed a Canadian fisheries bill which said that the convention of 1818, which permitted American vessels to enter British North American ports only for wood, water, shelter, and repairs, would be honored.

The United States was on the verge of passing a retaliatory bill, empowering the President to prevent Canadian ships from using American ports, except in case of distress. But Canada's firm stand in the matter seems to have impressed some American authorities, and in 1887 the American government, through its Secretary of State, invited Sir Charles Tupper and the prime minister, Sir John A. Macdonald, to discuss the fisheries question privately.

Macdonald accepted this unofficial invitation, and Tupper was dispatched to Washington to pay an informal call on the Secretary of State. A week after Tupper's return from Washington the Secretary of State wrote to Macdonald :

> I am confident we both seek to attain a just and permanent settlement, and there is but one way to procure it — and this is by a straightforward treatment on a liberal and statesmanlike plan of the entire commercial relations of the two countries.

Tupper's unofficial visit to Washington resulted in an agreement between England and the United States to appoint a joint high commission to settle outstanding Canadian-American disputes. Macdonald, who had been through the ordeal of the Washington Conference sixteen years earlier, began to worry about the appointment of a Canadian representative. He did not want to go himself, and he seems to have feared that Sir Charles Tupper could not be trusted to act alone. He also feared that the chairman of the British delegation, Joseph Chamberlain, would care little for Canada's views. No one was more concerned about the negotiations than the people of the Maritime provinces, many of whom made their living from the sea, and it is perhaps not surprising, therefore, that Archbishop O'Brien of Halifax wrote to the High Commissioner for Canada, Sir Charles Tupper, himself a maritimer, expressing his concern :

> Whilst I have but little confidence in Mr. Chamberlain, I have every hope that your knowledge of the importance of the question to the Maritime provinces and your desire for their prosperity, will more than compensate for the deficiency of the English represent- ative.

Macdonald worried over the terms of reference of the com- mission as well. Would they be broad enough to include commercial relations in general and the controversy over the Bering Sea, where the United States had been busily seizing Canadian sealing vessels and behaving as if the open ocean were an American resort ? He wanted the terms of reference to be as wide, and as explicit, as possible. When, in September of 1887, the terms of reference became known, Macdonald's worst fears seemed justified. Immensely annoyed, he wrote the Governor-General :

> *Dolus latet in generalibus* [in generalities lies grief] and the whole thing seems to be a snare laid by the United States government to entrap England into a commission to consider the expediency of relaxing the terms of the convention of 1818. This has long been their aim, and as it is the magna carta of the Maritimes provinces, must be resisted. You may think me suspicious, but I have a lively recollection of the manner in which the United States commissioners in 1871 at Washington, after getting the article settled respecting the Alabama claims, coolly refused to consider Canada's claim for Fenian invasions and outrages, on the ground that they were not authorized by the government.

On October 13, 1887, the Canadian cabinet decided to name Sir Charles Tupper as the Canadian representative at this new Washington conference, which began its meetings the following month. At the first meeting the Americans demanded the relaxation of the convention of 1818 regarding the fisheries. The British delegation refused, and in December they offered a counter-proposal : that the fishery privileges be revived in exchange for a Canadian-American tariff agreement. This time the United States refused. The meetings adjourned and Joseph Chamberlain, chairman of the British delegation, and Tupper went to Ottawa to consult the Canadian government. Before the conference met again the Canadian and British governments had worked out a plan whereby American fishing vessels could enter Canadian ports to buy supplies and to trans-ship fish if they had obtained a license from the Canadian government. The license fee would be based on tonnage. The plan also allowed for the waiver of the license fee if the Americans would repeal their duty on Canadian fish. What the plan did not include was provision for American vessels to obtain the privilege of fishing in Canadian territorial waters. It was the refusal to grant this privilege which almost made the conference end in disaster. When the Americans insisted on this privilege Chamberlain and Tupper exploded in anger. Tupper reported to Macdonald :

> (Chamberlain was) wildly indignant and he seems to have come to the conclusion that the American plenipotentiaries are a lot of dishonest tricksters.

The Canadian counsel, John Thompson, wrote to his wife :

> I am afraid nothing will come of our mission. These Yankee politicians are the lowest race of thieves in existence.

When Joseph Chamberlain threatened to return to England the conference settled down to a close examination of the Canadian proposal. Finally, on February 15, 1888, the commissioners agreed to a treaty. It would not have allowed free entry of Canadian fish into the United States, nor did the Americans agree to cease their fishing activities in the Bering Sea. However, they did agree to the establishment of a system of license fees in return for fishing privileges in Canadian coastal waters. This would have removed the main source of friction between the two governments, but when the treaty reached the U.S. Senate it was rejected there. And two days later President Cleveland, in a burst of chauvinism, sent a message to Congress, asking it to proclaim a state of complete commercial non-intercourse with Canada. Prime Minister Macdonald wrote to the Governor-General :

> Cleveland, I fancy, had ascertained that the Irish vote would carry New York against him, and so in desperation he took an extra twist at the tail of the British lion.

However, Cleveland's statement was nothing but bombast. Since the fishery question was too complex to be solved so easily, the Canadian position came to be more or less respected. For instance, the Canadian government continued to issue licences and American fishermen, by and large, accepted them. However, the failure of the negotiations of 1887 launched a campaign for closer ties with United States. The Liberal Party became convinced that Macdonald's insistence on the fisheries question had endangered Canada's commercial relations with the United States and felt that Canada's powerful neighbour had retaliated by increasing its protection to American products. This would mean a higher tariff and perhaps the collapse of the Canadian economy. And so, the Liberal Party proposed that the time had come to tell the Americans that the Canadian destiny was clearly linked to theirs. Wilfrid Laurier so stated on August 27, 1888 in St. Thomas, Ontario :

> Again I say it is high time we reversed our policy towards the United States. After all blood is thicker than water. Those who live on the other side of the line come from the British Isles as most of us do. Those who live on the other side of the line have the same literature and the same language. The time has come when there should be closer relations. Let us remain as we are politically, but let us agree that it would be for their benefit, and for our benefit, that there should be no customs laws, but that we should exchange our produce from one side of the line to the other. This is the policy of the Liberal party. For my part I believe that we look no longer on them with jealousy, that we are glad of their success, that we are sincere friends and brothers, and that we would have no difficulty in arriving at the subject we have in view.

Three years after Laurier made that speech, Prime Minister Macdonald was dead, having fought the last campaign of his political life on the issue of closer ties with Great Britain rather than with the United States. In the quarter of a century during which he was responsible for Canada's relations both with Great Britain and the United States, he was able to demonstrate clearly that Canada was an imperial and international fact. Indeed, he made possible Canada's entry into the society of free and independant nations. As usual, Macdonald pointed the way which others followed.

# CANADA TO THE WOLVES (III)  12
## External Affairs Under Laurier

Wilfrid Laurier was elected Prime Minister of Canada in 1896. He had been defeated in an earlier attempt, in 1891, when he ran on a platform which advocated a reciprocal trade agreement with the United States. The British North American colonies had had such an agreement with their neighbour for about 10 years prior to Confederation. Its abrogation in 1865 was a blow to the economy of British North America, and was in fact, one of the economic causes of Confederation — the union of the colonies into the Dominion of Canada.

Lack of a trade agreement with the United States caused much hardship in the new nation to the north, and the "National Policy" of the first prime minister, Sir John A. Macdonald, had not proved as beneficial to the economy as he had hoped it would. Macdonald had tried to bolster Canada's economy by protecting its industries with tariffs, by building a national railway, and by encouraging settlement of the west. But many believed that in spite of his efforts Canada was stagnating economically.

Nevertheless, whenever someone advocated a renewal of reciprocity with the United States as a solution to Canada's economic problems, there were always others who saw in such plans the first steps towards political union, towards "annexation".

For example, in 1887 the Liberal Party, then the opposition party in Parliament, officially adopted a policy of reciprocity with the United States as its most important plank. Wilfrid Laurier, leader of the party, explained that it was natural and normal for a colony to attempt to loosen the bonds which tied it to the Mother Country:

> It was our hope at one time to make this country a nation. It is our hope yet. [I hail that sentiment with joy, with unbounded joy, all the more that it is altogether unforeseen. I had expected, from the talk we have heard from these gentlemen on the other side of the House, that they expected that this country would forever and forever remain a colony. I see now that they have higher aspirations, and I give them credit for that.] Colonies are destined to become nations, as it is the destiny of a child to become a man. No one [, even on the other side,] will assume that this country, which will some day number a larger population than Great Britain, is forever to remain in its present political relation with Great Britain. The time is coming when the present relations of Great Britain and Canada must either become closer or be severed altogether ... "If ever and whenever Canada chooses", to use the language of Lord Palmerston, "to stand by herself, the separation will take place not only in peace but in friendship and in love, as the son leaves the house of his father to become himself the father of a family."

To Laurier, reciprocity with the United States would lead to increasing independence from Great Britain, but not to annexation to the United States.

The fact that it was Laurier's Liberals who advocated reciprocity with the United States does not mean that all the Conservatives opposed a trade agreement with that country. The Conservative Prime Minister, Sir John A. Macdonald, had in fact made many overtures in the past to the United States government for a reciprocity treaty, and late in 1890 a new opportunity came when the U.S. Secretary of State invited the Canadian government to discuss trade relations with him. Sir John wrote to his Minister of Justice :

> We have held in Parliament and elsewhere that our attempts to negotiate had been so often rejected by the United States that we could not in self-respect go on our knees again, but that we were ready, whenever the United States might make any sign of a desire to negotiate, to go into the matter honestly. This suggestion of the American Secretary of State gives us the opportunity and will prevent the opposition from stating that we have abandoned our ground and taken up theirs.

So the Canadian government despatched a brief statement of its proposal to Washington and London, but the Americans said they could not receive the Canadian representatives for several months.

Then a curious thing happened. The American Secretary of State gave an interview to one of the editors of the Toronto *Globe,* on the subject of Canadian-American trade. On the same day he also denied that there were any negotiations going on with Canada. He wrote to a congressman who had inquired about the subject:

> I authorize you to contradict the rumours you refer to. There are no negotiations whatever on foot for a reciprocity treaty with Canada. We know nothing of Sir Charles Tupper coming to Washington.

Macdonald was furious. The Canadian government had been made a fool of. The old man decided to retaliate. He knew that the Liberals would fight the election that year, 1891, on a platform of unrestricted reciprocity with the United States. He would give them the kind of fight they were asking for.

And so it came about that Macdonald, who had willingly agreed to discuss a reciprocal trade agreement with the United States, became a violent opponent of reciprocity in the election of 1891. He pictured the entire commercial union movement as a gigantic plot to impoverish the people of Canada. and bring about annexation. In Halifax he said:

> I say that there is a deliberate conspiracy in which some of the members of the opposition are more or less compromised. I say that there is a deliberate conspiracy, by force, by fraud, or by both, to force Canada into the American union.

"The old man, the old flag, and the old policy" became the slogan of the Conservatives in the election campaign of 1891. Macdonald's entire campaign can be summed up by his statement:

A British subject I was born, a British subject I will die. With my utmost strength, with my last breath will I oppose the veiled treason which attempts, by sordid means and mercenary proffers, to lure our people from their allegiance.

By March 5, 1891, the Canadian people seem to have been convinced that unrestricted reciprocity with the United States, as advocated by the Liberals, did mean annexation in the long run. For they returned Macdonald to power. But Macdonald was not to enjoy his victory for long. Within three months he was dead. After his death the Conservative party went into a rapid decline, and by 1896, the year of the next election, it was generally discredited. Wilfrid Laurier came to power in his second attempt at the Canadian leadership.

Once Laurier was in power, it became obvious how absurd had been the charges of disloyalty to the Empire levelled against him during the election campaign. Laurier was animated by respect for the political principles that Great Britain seemed to represent. Many years earlier, in Quebec City, in the heart of French Canada, Laurier had expressed his admiration for British political institutions. Neither France nor French Canada, but England, was the source of his political ideals, he said. Laurier was essentially a 19th century liberal who believed in the right of private property, free trade, and the sanctity of individual rights. However, much as he admired English institutions and the ideal of a commonwealth of free nations within the Empire, it was the ideal of national unity that was closest to Laurier's heart. Most of all, he wanted French Canadians and English Canadians to know each other, to understand each other, and to forget the quarrels which had divided them in the past. In 1899, Canada sent troops to fight in the Boer War. It did so reluctantly, under pressure from the Governor-General and from the "jingoists" — the imperial extremists. In his farewell to the soldiers embarking at Quebec City, Laurier seized the opportunity to point out the advantages to Canadian unity which would result from participation in the war in South Africa :

In wishing you God-speed I pray that God may accompany you, direct you and protect you on the noble mission which you have undertaken. Upon this occasion it is not so much the God of battle as the God of justice whom we invoke.

This is an unique occasion in the history of the world; it is a spectacle which ought to make every Canadian feel proud of his country. Who could have believed a few years ago that from this city, which had been the theatre of bitter conflict between the two proudest races of the world, their descendants, who to-day are a happy and united people, would go forth to help carry the blessings of their own institutions to a far distant land ? Who could have believed thirty-two years ago that the scattered provinces of British North America would have reached such a point of development today that they would be able and willing, and cheerfully willing, to cement with their blood the unity of the Empire in its most distant part ?

Should any one of you unfortunately lose life or limb, your country will feel that you have fully discharged the duty under which you place her this day by this sacrifice to Canada's glory, the glory of the Empire, and, above all, to the cause of justice, humanity, and liberty.

However, devoted though he was to the cause of "the Empire, justice, humanity, and liberty", Laurier found almost all of his time devoted to working out everyday problems of Canada's relations with its great neighbour, the United States. When he took power in 1896, not a single old issue involving Canadian-American relations had been completely settled, and new ones constantly loomed on the horizon. Among the old and new issues were those concerning American fishing rights in Canadian coastal waters, the rights of Canadian sealing vessels in the Bering Sea, and the lack of a treaty respecting the transporting of goods across the border in bond to a sea port or to another part of the country or origin. There were also difficulties over the movement of Canadian workers to the United States, over armed vessels on the Great Lakes, and over the discovery of gold in the Klondike. The latter difficulty was to create the most important problem of all : the settlement of the vast Alaska-Canada boundary.

Unfortunately, however, the atmosphere was not conducive to a frank and friendly discussion of the various issues. There existed at this time in the United States a feeling of assurance in the "American way of life" which disturbed the Canadians. When the Americans talked about their "manifest destiny" and "our continent", the Canadians worried.

Once in power, the Liberal party, under Laurier, was committed to ironing out the difficulties between the two countries. During his first year in office, Laurier met with no success. The Americans refused to discuss reciprocity, and in fact, in 1897, they imposed the highest tariff in the annals of American protection. Matters did not begin to look up until March of 1898, when Laurier had been in office for two years. Then the United States agreed to discuss the possibility of a mixed commission to settle mutual problems. Two months later a joint high commission was established.

The commission met, off and on, in Quebec City and Washington for about 18 weeks toward the end of 1898 and the beginning of 1899. It was not a complete failure, but it did fail to settle the main problem — that of the Canada-Alaska boundary. Here is how Laurier outlined the achievements and failures of the meetings, in a letter to a friend :

> There has been a great deal of misconception as to the character of the negotiations at Washington. The impression was that we were struggling with might and main to obtain a wide measure of reciprocity. The reverse is the truth. [We struggled to obtain reciprocity in lumber, because the condition of things in so far as lumber is concerned is acute and may become worse. I may say, however, that in this we made no progress whatever. We also endeavoured to obtain a fair measure of reciprocity in minerals, in which we were altogether successful; in quarry products, in which we were also quite successful; and in a few agricultural products in which we had some partial success.] On the whole with reference to the reciprocity question, I am quite satisfied with the progress which we made, [barring the sole article of lumber,] and we can at any moment make a very fair treaty. Our chief efforts, however, were directed to three subjects : the Atlantic fisheries, the Pacific seal fisheries, and the Alaska boundary. [With regard to the Atlantic fisheries, we made no progress whatever. Concerning the Pacific seal fisheries, we would have obtained a very valuable treaty. Efforts have been made, as you know, to discredit our action on this subject as implying a surrender of national rights. As to this, the seal fishermen are the best judges, and we kept ourselves, at every step, in close contact with them. I have no hesitation to say thåt the arrangement that we would have made, and with which they were satisfied, would have been acceptable to the whole country and would have shown that we made no surrender.]
>
> The stumbling-block was the Alaska boundary. In this, our American fellow Commissioners were at first and almost to the last disposed to come to a reasonable compromise. I may tell

> you confidentially that the compromise was that they gave us Pyramid Harbour on the Lynn Canal with everything but the official sovereignty in name; in other words, the arrangement which we had practically concluded was that we should have Pyramid Harbour under our jurisdiction, our laws and our administration, but that if, at any moment, we chose no longer to occupy it, it would revert to the United States. This arrangement provoked such a storm in the Pacific states that our fellow Commissioners withdrew their consent. There was nothing left but to arbitrate.

However, the American representatives would not accept the Canadians' proposal as to the method of arbitration. As Laurier concluded :

> There was nothing else to do but stop then and there. They offered to go on with the other subjects referred to us, but this we declined to do, and insisted, before we proceeded with the other articles, that they should either settle the boundary question by agreement or by reference to arbitration.

Here is the background to the Canada-Alaska boundary dispute: The United States had bought Alaska from Russia in 1867 under the terms of the Anglo-Russian treaty of 1825. But that treaty had been framed without an accurate knowledge of the country in question. What was important for Canada, especially for the province of British Columbia, was that northern development should not be hampered. The Alaska boundary dispute came to a head after 1898, with the influx of gold seekers in the gold rush of those years, especially in the Klondike region. What Canada needed was an outlet to the sea.

The area under dispute was the Alaska "panhandle", that strip of land which extends south along the Pacific Ocean and joins the province of British Columbia. The Anglo-Russian Treaty of 1825 had defined the boundary as forming a line parallel to the mountains where there were some within ten marine leagues from the sea, and parallel to the coastline where there were no mountains. The United States insisted that there were no mountains ten marine leagues from the sea, and that the boundary should therefore be drawn 10 marine leagues inland. This would have deprived the northern part of British Columbia and the Yukon of access to the sea.

After the breakdown of negotiations at the meetings of the Joint High Commission of 1898 and 1899 the Americans proposed a tribunal of six — half British and half American. This was unacceptable to Canada, and Sir Wilfrid Laurier was determined not to give way. However, in March 1902, he was forced to reconsider when President Theodore Roosevelt sent troops to southern Alaska. There was no doubt in anyone's mind that he was prepared to use force if necessary to get his way. England could not possibly contemplate war with the United States over the Alaska boundary and forced Canada to accept the six-member commission proposed by the United States.

Consequently in January 1903, Great Britain and the United States signed a treaty agreeing to a board of six international jurists of impartiality and great repute. The United States was most apprehensive. It feared the word "impartiality". If a majority decision was to be reached one member of the commission would have to vote against his own country. However, President Roosevelt was not worried that any of his commissioners would do that. In his characteristic fashion he stated that he had accepted the arbitration only :

... to enable Great Britain to save her face.

President Roosevelt also sent a letter to a prominent American in which he left no doubt as to the American position :

If there is a disagreement, I wish it distinctly understood not only that there will be no arbitration of the matter, but that in my message to Congress I shall take a position which will prevent any possibility of arbitration hereafter; a position ... which will render it necessary for Congress to give me the authority to run the line as we claim it, by our own people, without any further regard to the attitude of England and Canada. If I paid attention to mere abstract rights, that is the position I ought to take anyhow. I have not taken it because I wish to exhaust every effort to have the affair settled peacefully and with due regard to England's honor.

The American members appointed to the "impartial" tribunal were Mr. Elihu Root, Senator Henry Cabot Lodge, and Senator Turner.

Turner was from the state of Washington which did very well on the Yukon trade. Mr. Root was the Secretary of War who had been responsible for the supervision of the dispatch of

American troops to Alaska in 1902. And Senator Lodge was an Anglophobe who had once described the Canadian case as :

... Baseless, and a manufactured claim.

Once these appointments were made the United States Congress ratified the treaty agreeing to the arbitration of the Canada-Alaska boundary dispute. The Canadian government was aghast, but there was not much it could do, especially when England, without waiting for Canada's comments, also ratified the treaty. Canada's case was to be presented by the Chief Justice of England, Lord Alverstone, who was to serve as head of the delegation; Louis A. Jetté, the Lieutenant-Governor of Quebec; and A.B. Aylesworth, a leader of the Ontario bar, who was later to become Canada's Minister of Justice. Unlike the American delegation, the Canadian delegation was not a unified group. It consisted of representatives of two different countries with different aspirations and interests. Canada wanted its outlet to the sea; England wanted to avoid war with the United States. Lord Alverstone soon began to create difficulties for the Canadian delegates, as this cable to Laurier from a member of the Canadian delegation demonstrates :

I think that the Chief Justice intends joining the Americans, deciding in such a way as to defeat us on every point. We all think that the Chief Justice's intentions are unjustifiable and due to predetermination to avoid trouble with the United States. Jetté and Aylesworth are much exasperated and considering withdrawing from the commission.

Prime Minister Laurier replied :

If we are thrown over by the Chief Justice he will give the last blow to British diplomacy in Canada.

The worst fears of the Canadians were proved well founded when, following an initial period of deadlock, Lord Alverstone voted with the Americans. The United States was given an unbroken strip nearly as wide as she had claimed, and two of the four islands at the mouth of the important Portland Canal, leading into the British Columbia interior. The Canadian delegates Jetté and Aylesworth refused to sign, but it was only a token protest. The thing was done.

Reaction in Canada was one of deep humiliation, anger and frustration. Once more Canada felt betrayed and offered up as sacrifice on the altar of Anglo-American friendship. With unusual vigour, Prime Minister Laurier stated in Parliament :

> What are we to do ? I have often regretted, Mr. Speaker, and never more than on the present occasion, that we are living beside a great neighbour who, I believe I can say without being deemed unfriendly to them, are very grasping in their national actions, and who are determined on every occasion to get the best of any agreement which they make. I have often regretted also that while they are a great and powerful nation, we are only a small colony, a growing colony, but still a colony. I have often regretted also that we have not in our hands the treaty-making power which would enable us to dispose of our own affairs. Our hands are tied to a large extent, owing to the fact of our connection — which has its benefits, but which also has its disadvantages — the fact of our connection with the mother country making us not free agents and obliging us to deal with questions affecting ourselves through the instrumentality of British ambassadors...
> [The difficulty as I conceive it is not there (with Lord Alverstone).] The difficulty as I conceive it to be, is that so long as Canada remains a dependency of the British Crown the present powers that we have are not sufficient for the maintenance of our rights. It is important that we should ask the British parliament for more extensive powers so that if ever we have to deal with matters of a similar nature again, we shall deal with them in our own way, in our own fashion, according to the best light that we have.

If, in so speaking, Laurier was outlining future Canadian policy, it was not implemented at that time. The fury had its day, and then, as usual, tempers began to cool down.

It must be admitted that most experts agree that the United States had the better case. The Canadian position would never have been upheld in any court.

The Alaska boundary incident was one of those diplomatic incidents which satisfies nobody. The United States had little use for a strip of territory which was made up largely of decaying mines and of an impenetrable wilderness. England reconciled herself with the Americans at the price of Canadian discontent. And once more Canada feared American expansionism.

The incident is also important because it helped to re-assert Canadian nationalism. But it was a queer type of nationalism in that it involved a determination to establish direct communication between the United States and Canada without weakening the Imperial attachment.

Canada's proposal to deal directly with the United States was well received by the Americans. President Roosevelt wrote to Mr. Root, his Secretary of War, that negotiations with Canada should be handled by a special minister to Canada, even if this meant, in Roosevelt's words :

> ... a reversal of the policy that would have to obtain were England's control of Canada absolute.

Two years later, young William Lyon Mackenzie King, who was one day to be Prime Minister of Canada, went to Washington to discuss with the President problems arising out of Asiatic immigration to Canada.

Another precedent was set in 1909 when an International Joint Commission was created to deal with the problems of boundary waters. Even though the treaty creating the commission was signed by the British representative, the British government had absolutely no control over, and no voice in, the activities of the Commission.

The same year Canada also created its own Department of External Affairs. It began modestly, situated over a barbershop in Ottawa. It had a staff of three and an annual budget of $13,000. Laurier explained the decision to create such a department as follows :

> All governments have found it necessary to have a department whose only business shall be to deal with relations with foreign countries, and in our judgment Canada has reached a period in her history when we should follow the example of other countries in that respect, as for example, the Commonwealth of Australia ... We have given this matter a good deal of consideration and the conclusion we have arrived at is that the foreign affairs with which Canada has to deal are becoming of such absorbing moment as to necessitate special machinery.

Such were the beginnings of Canada's involvement in international affairs. From that time onwards such activities increased considerably.

In time, Canada would no longer be thrown to the wolves, except by her own choice.

# "THE INSPIRATION AND THE HOPE"
## Canada on the Eve of the First World War

In the first decade of the 20th century it became quite apparent that the various conflicts of interests in Europe would in time cause war. Most nations appeared unable to rise above their petty jealousies and emerge from their nationalistic ghettos in the pursuance of policies which could be internationally accepted, and maintain the peace which everyone was so keen, at least in theory, to preserve. The only solution which appeared to the weak and senseless men in power was recourse to a rigid militarism and the building up of vast supplies of armaments.

To Britain, Germany stood as the main culprit since, because of its determination and efficiency, it seemed destined to outclass England on the high seas. England, with her naval tradition and prestige, and her utter reliance on sea power as a means of defense, could not tolerate any rival. Pressure at home for the maintenance of a strong and powerful navy spread to the colonies, who were urged to assist England in the gigantic undertaking.

Canada did not respond as quickly as some had wanted. Canadians, so far from Europe, were quite ignorant of the issues and struggles which went on constanly on that continent. Many were optimistic enough to believe that sanity would in the long run prevail. How well this view was expressed by the Postmaster-General, Sir William Mulock, in 1906 when he said :

> This Canada of ours is the only country in the world worth living in that is not burdened with great military debts. Keep it on those lines ... Remember that this is the last spot of refuge on God's green earth where men can come and pay tribute for the sins of their ancestors.

However, three years later, the Canadian parliament adopted a resolution that a Canadian navy be created. The motion came first from a Conservative party member on the Opposition side of the House of Commons, who insisted that Canada's own coastlines should be protected by Canada's own navy. The British government had insisted that the Empire should have a single navy under her command, but the Canadians felt that they, as a self-governing people, should not be required to contribute funds to the British government.

The Conservative member's motion was upheld by the Liberal Prime Minister Laurier. Then Laurier moved his own motion for a Canadian naval force. The Opposition assented and the following resolution was adopted without division :

> This House fully recognizes the duty of the people of Canada, as they increase in numbers and wealth, to assume in larger measure the responsibilities in national defence.
>
> The House is of the opinion that under the present constitutional relations between the Mother Country and the self-governing Dominions, the payment of regular and periodical contributions to the Imperial treasury for naval and military purposes would not, so far as Canada is concerned, be the most satisfactory solution to the question of defence.
>
> The House will cordially approve of any necessary expenditure designed to promote the speedy organization of a Canadian naval service in cooperation with and in close relation to the Imperial Navy, along the lines suggested by the Admiralty at the last Imperial

Conference, and in full sympathy with the view that the naval supremacy of Britain is essential to the security of commerce, the safety of the Empire and the peace of the world.

The House expresses its firm conviction that whenever the need arises the Canadian people will be found ready and willing to make any sacrifice that is required to give the Imperial authorities the most loyal and hearty cooperation in every movement for the maintenance of the integrity and honour of the Empire.

In July of that year, 1909, an Imperial Conference adopted a resolution bearing on the construction of individual navies for the colonies which desired them. The Canadian Naval Service Bill was introduced in January 1910. The Bill provided for the establishment of a Canadian navy which in time of emergency could be placed at the disposal of the British Government *should the Canadian Parliament sanction such a move*. Laurier defended his position as being a middle of the road one. He chastised the Imperial extremists as men who :

... carry abroad upon their foreheads Imperial phylacteries, who boldly walk into the temple and there loudly thank the Lord that they are not like other British subjects, that they give tithes of everything they possess, and that in them alone is to be found the true incense of loyalty.

He refused to admit that there existed a state of emergency with Germany. He insisted that Canada had to remain master in its own house. On the other hand he felt that Canada had to do something. Those who insisted that nothing should be done were blind, for as Laurier stated :

There sit the two extremes, side by side, cheek by jowl, blowing hot and cold. I have dealt with those who blow hot; let me try a word now with those who blow cold. They say we have no mandate, that our policy has never been discussed. Have they not read time and again the memorandum submitted to the Imperial Conference of 1902 ? And Canada has progressed since 1902. Did these men forget that Canada is a country with two sea-coasts, and exposed coast cities, a country with a large ocean trade, with abounding national revenues ? You might as well tell the people of Montreal, with their half-million population, that they do not need any police protection.

He wanted all to remember that :

If England is at war, we are at war and liable to attack. I do not say that we shall always be attacked, neither do I say that we would take part in all the wars of England. This is a matter that must be guided by circumstances, upon which the Canadian Parliament will have to pronounce, and will have to decide in its own best judgement.

The opposition to his plan came from two sources : those Conservatives who felt that not enough was being done for the Empire, and certain French Canadians who disapproved of a naval establishment on the grounds that it would mean immediate and automatic participation in wars of the Empire. The opposition of the Conservatives is interesting because the previous year they had agreed with Laurier that Canada should and must have its own navy. Laurier once assessed the validity of the opposition to his project. He wrote to an old friend :

> We are, without doubt, in for a little agitation on the part of the Nationalists and Conservatives, who are at last uniting in a solid party. So far I have no serious apprehension. I am quite aware that our policy is not popular; for all that I do not think that they can fool the public about it. The only effect that I foresee is that it is going to consolidate the Opposition in the province of Quebec and probably divide it in the Dominion; I believe that on the whole all the same elements will stay with us, and if so, we have nothing to fear.

> The clerical journals have already seized on the question to make a breach in our ranks. It seems to me that this is an obvious blunder and at the proper moment we must fall on them and tell them to their faces that this is an abuse of religion.

To a senator of his own party who objected to the expense involved in the building of the navy, and who felt that Canada should merely give Great Britain dreadnoughts, Laurier wrote :

> I am shocked and scandalized at your attitude. I always knew you to be a Grit and a Reformer belonging to the party which, from the time of William Lyon Mackenzie, insisted that we should have the handling of our own affairs. We claim that at this stage we have reached the status of a nation, at least I do. All nations must have a navy as well as an army, but I tell you frankly that I do not intend the Canadian army or navy to be on a scale to threaten the peace of the world.

> I have not missed the passage in your letter in which you attribute the attitude we have taken to representations from Quebec. I have read that in the Tory press, but was not prepared to see it from the pen of an old Grit. The Tory press is doing its very best to create a prejudice and a cleavage between Quebec and the rest of the Dominion. This is not new : it is as old as the history of Canada under British rule. It has failed before and will fail again.

Unfortunately the matter could not be dismissed so lightly. It formed an important issue in the elections of 1911, and it contributed to the defeat of the Laurier government. The Liberals were replaced by the Conservatives and Prime Minister Wilfrid Laurier by Robert Laird Borden. Borden was in many ways a worthy leader in the tradition of Laurier and Sir John A. Macdonald. He was fair and honest, a determined foe of injustice, a keen observer of the Canadian scene, and a well-known constitutional authority. He had great patience and persistence and a tremendous capacity for work.

In the summer of 1912, the new prime minister went to England and came immediately under the strong and persuasive influence of a young man by the name of Winston Churchill. Before he returned to Canada, he had made up his mind. He said :

> The supremacy of the seas must be maintained by one navy under one central control and direction.

[He thus agreed with Churchill who had said in May of 1912 :

> If the main development of the last ten years has been the concentration of the British fleet in decisive theatres, it seems to me not unlikely that the main naval development of the next ten years will be the growth of effective naval forces in the great Dominions over seas ... The fact that our fleet has not only concentrated in the decisive theatre of European waters, but must be kept concentrated and in a certain sense tied to that theatre has been for some years creating a new situation, a new need, a new opportunity for the great self-governing Dominions of the Crown.]

On December 5, 1912, Borden introduced his Navy Aid Bill and launched one of the longest, most implacable and most famous debates since Confederation. The bill provided for $35,000,000 to build three dreadnoughts in Great Britain. The ships would be placed at the disposal of the British navy and Canada could recall them when the situation permitted. The government's case was put by Borden himself :

> The next ten or twenty years will be pregnant with great results for this Empire; and it is of infinite importance that questions of purely domestic concern, however urgent, shall not prevent any of us from rising 'to the height of this great argument'. But today, while the clouds are heavy and we hear the booming of

the distant thunder and see the lightning flashes above the horizon, we cannot and we will not wait and deliberate until any impending storm shall have burst upon us in fury and with disaster. Almost unaided, the Motherland, not for herself alone, but for us as well, is sustaining the burden of a vital Imperial duty, and confronting an overmastering necessity of national existence. Bringing the best assistance that we may in the urgency of the moment, we come thus to her aid, in token of our determination to protect and ensure the safety and integrity of this Empire, and of our resolve to defend on sea as well as on land our flag, our honour and our heritage.

From the other side of the House of Commons, Sir Wilfrid Laurier, prime minister the previous year, now the Leader of the Opposition, energetically battled the government :

What is this contribution that we have to-day before us, and upon which we are asked to vote ? [It is big in omen; it is big in figures. Is it as big otherwise as it ought to be ?] I ask every honourable member of this House; I ask every honourable gentleman sitting there : You give England two or three dreadnoughts, to be paid for by Canada, but to be equipped, maintained and manned by England. Did I say manned by England ? I must qualify that statement. In justice to my right honourable friend, I must qualify that statement; because he told us that he had secured from the Imperial authorities the privilege of having Canadian officers serve on those ships. Oh, ye Tory jingoes ! Is that the amount of the sacrifice you are prepared to make ? You are ready to furnish admirals, rear-admirals, commodores, captains, officers of all grades, plumes, feathers, and gold lace; but you leave it to England to supply the bone and sinews on board those ships. You say that these ships shall bear Canadian names. That will be the only thing Canadian about them. You hire somebody to do your work; in other words, you are ready to do anything except the fighting. Is that, sir, the true policy ?

(*Some honourable members : No. No !*)

Is that the true policy ? It is a hybrid policy; it is a cross between jingoism and nationalism. Unless I mistake the spirit of the Canadian people, if they are true to their ideals, if they are true to their own blood, no matter to what province they belong, they will not be satisfied with this hybrid policy, but they will insist that their contribution shall be a contribution of money and of men as well ...

The Bill introduced in the Commons in December of 1912 was not passed until May 15, 1913 and only after the government had introduced the parliamentary device called "closure" to end the debate and silence the opposition. Borden then sent the bill to the Senate where a Liberal majority defeated it on May 29. An attempt to compromise was not successful and the matter was shelved temporarily. Borden had the audacity to suggest to the Imperial government that it go ahead and build the dreadnoughts and that before their completion he would induce parliament to pay for them. The Imperial authorities rightly enough refused to have anything to do with such an anti-constitutional and anti-parliamentary procedure. The result of Borden's inability to compromise and his refusal to cope with the realities of his era was that when the war broke out in August of 1914, Canada had no navy. As its naval war effort Canada formed a small coast guard navy and sent men into the British navy. The price of Borden's political foolishness was indeed great.

However there was not much outcry at the time of the rejection of the bill. The reason for this was that Canadians were perturbed by the economic situation. The boom which had endured until roughly 1907 had come to an end. Only reciprocity with the United States could have offset it. Unfortunately this did not become a reality in 1911 and so the economy continued to decline. The end of the great era meant a tightening of credit with the usual results : construction halted, factories slowed down, and unemployment mounted. Even though the Liberal opposition made capital of these difficulties by insisting that Laurier meant prosperity and Borden depression, Borden could not be blamed.

The most important effect of what turned out to be a temporary depression was its effect upon railway development. By the time Laurier left office, there were railways everywhere; some of them even ran nowhere. It was soon apparent that not much foresight and planning had gone into this vast railway system. Millions and millions of dollars had been spent, and spent with not much to show for them except rusty tracks and economic chaos. It soon became imperative to lend money to the various companies, to refloat their loans and insure their credit. Borden's government was reluctant but something had to be done.

On May 13, 1914, the government introduced its resolutions to help the Canadian Northern Railway systems. Canada was to become proprietor of this transcontinental railway for a sum of roughly 40 million dollars. After much debate the government's proposals were accepted by the House. A few weeks later the government granted financial assistance to the Grand Trunk Railway and the Grand Trunk Pacific Railway. And with that Parliament adjourned on June 12, 1914.

Towards the end of July telegrams on the European situation began to pour in. Borden had felt in 1912 that war was really inevitable. He never parted from that view. Sixteen days after the adjournment of the Canadian Houses of Parliament, news had come of the assassination of Archduke Franz Ferdinand at Sarajevo on June 28, 1914. The world awaited events with anxiety and fear. By the end of July there was really no doubt that this was to be more than a Balkan war and that Britain was likely to be involved : Borden wired the British government the following :

> My advisers while expressing their most earnest hope that peaceful solution of existing international difficulties may be achieved and their strong desire to co-operate in every possible way for that purpose wish me to convey to His Majesty's Government the firm assurance that if unhappily war should ensue the Canadian people will be united in common resolve to put forth every effort and to make every sacrifice necessary to ensure the integrity and maintain the honour of our Empire.

At 8:55 p.m. on August 4th, 1914, a telegram arrived announcing that war had been declared. Parliament was summoned for August 18. Borden wrote in his memoirs :

> Although the events of the past few days had quite prepared us for this result, it came at the last as a shock. None of us, at that time, anticipated the terrible duration of the war agony; but we did realize that the struggle would be intense. It was difficult to retain one's balance in the unexpected and bewildering environment that had enveloped us in what seemed but a moment.

It was with great difficulty that Borden could tell the members of Parliament :

... The future is shrouded in uncertainty, but I believe that the people of Canada look forth upon it with steadfast eyes. But, while we are now upborne by the exaltation and enthusiasm which come in the first days of a national crisis, so great that it moves the hearts of all men, we must not forget that days may come when our patience, our endurance and our fortitude will be tried to the utmost. In those days let us see to it that no heart grows faint and that no courage be found wanting.

And after having reviewed governmental action to prepare for the war, he concluded :

It is not fitting that I should prolong this debate. In the awful dawn of the greatest war the world has ever known, in the hour when peril confronts us, such as this Empire has not faced for a hundred years, every vain or unnecessary word seems a discord. As to our duty, all are agreed, we stand shoulder to shoulder with Britain and the other British Dominions in this quarrel. And that duty we shall not fail to fulfil as the honour of Canada demands. Not for love of battle, not for lust of conquest, not for greed of possessions, but for the cause of honour, to maintain solemn pledges, to uphold principles of liberty, to withstand forces that would convert the world into an armed camp; yea, in the very name of the peace that we sought at any cost save that of dishonour, we have entered into this war; and while gravely conscious of the tremendous issues involved and of all the sacrifices that they may entail, we do not shrink from them, but with firm hearts we abide the event.

If it was painful for Borden, it was even more so for Laurier, that supreme example of a man of peace and moderation and tolerance. Laurier understood what the war would mean more than anyone else. It did not mean to him a return to prosperity or anything of the sort. It meant essentially that men had lost their minds and in the process of redressing their wicked deeds young men, women and children would die.

On the horizon he also saw — and how well he knew it from personal experience in peacetime — that passions would be stirred and that the war effort might well mean the straining if not the destruction of that national unity he had laboured so long to establish and maintain. On August 19, 1914 he brought the command of his amazing oratory to bear on the awsome moment that the world, his country, and his people faced :

England to-day is not engaged in an ordinary contest. The war in which she is engaged will in all probability — nay in absolute certainty — stagger the world with its magnitude and its horror. But that war is for as noble a cause as ever impelled a nation to risk her all upon the arbitrament of the sword. That question is no longer at issue; the judgment of the world has already pronounced upon it.

Today the allied nations are fighting for freedom against oppression, for democracy against autocracy, for civilization against reversion to that state of barbarism in which the supreme law is the law of might.

Canada's entry into the First World War was, of course, violently opposed by certain groups of French Canadians, for the same reason that they had opposed Canada's entry into the Boer War fifteen years earlier : They did not see why Canada should be called upon to fight Britain's wars for her. To them, Laurier addressed a special word :

If my words can be heard beyond the walls of this House in the province from which I come, among the men whose blood flows in my own veins, I should like them to remember that in taking their place to-day in the ranks of the Canadian army to fight for the cause of the allied nations, a double honour rests upon them. The very cause for which they are called upon to fight is to them doubly sacred.

Sir, there is in this the inspiration and the hope that from this painful war the British Empire will emerge with a new bond of union, the pride of all its citizens, and a living light to all other nations.